Praise and Peanut Butter
a devotional cookbook
for college

By Stacey Roberts
author of 'Hotcakes and Hallelujahs' and the upcoming 'Manna at Midday'

Praise and Peanut Butter, A Devotional Cookbook

Copyright © 2015 by Stacey Roberts

All rights reserved, except as permitted under the U.S. Copyright Act of 1976. No parts of this publication may be reproduced, distributed or transmitted in any form or by any means, or stored in a data base or retrieval system, except for brief quotations in printed reviews, without the prior written permission of the publisher.

Scripture quotations marked NIV are from The Holy Bible, New International Version®, (NIV®) Copyright © 1973, 1978, 1984, 2011 by Biblica, Inc.™ Used by permission. All rights reserved worldwide. Fair use clause.

Scripture quotations marked ESV are from The Holy Bible, English Standard Version® (ESV®), copyright © 2001 by Crossway, a publishing ministry of Good News Publishers. Used by permission. All rights reserved.

Scripture quotations marked NLT are taken from the Holy Bible, New Living Translation, copyright © 1996, 2004, 2007 by Tyndale House Foundation. Used by permission of Tyndale House Publishers, Inc., Carol Stream, Illinois 60188. All rights reserved.

Scripture quotations marked KJV are from The Holy Bible, King James Version.

Photos throughout this book have been licensed through Shutterstock or are of our own creation, all rights reserved. Cover photo from Shutterstock.

Copyright 2015

For Mark, Matthew, Kathryne, Riley and Emma.

My backpack overfloweth.

Devotions

Feed Your Mind and Your Spirit

After three days they found him in the temple courts, sitting among the teachers, listening to them and asking them questions.
Luke 2:46 NIV

Congratulations! You did it! You worked hard in high school, graduated, passed the entrance exams and moved away from home to start your new life as a college student. Now what?

Are you going to jump right into campus life, participate in every activity, go to every football game, every concert, every party? Are you going to focus on your school work, attend every lecture, every study group and graduate with honors?

College is full of new experiences. Not all of the lessons you learn will occur in a classroom. You will learn how to live with roommates (not always easy), how to budget your time, how to feed yourself, how to say no to certain temptations and to say yes to doing your homework.

Jesus loved learning. He sought it out. When He was a boy He went to the temple so that He could learn from the priests. He was so engrossed with what they had to say that He lost track of time and did not return home when He was supposed to. His parents looked for Him for three days and when they found Him, He was still sitting among the teachers, listening and asking questions. He craved knowledge.

Now that you have this wonderful opportunity to learn, will you make it a priority? Today, ask God to help you keep your focus on Him and on the real task at hand. And when your work is done, go out there and have some fun!

Do Clothes Really Make the (Wo)Man?

*Therefore, as God's chosen people, holy and
dearly loved, clothe yourselves with compassion,
kindness, humility, gentleness and patience.
Colossians 3:12 NIV*

Every day you wake up, get dressed, comb your hair and present yourself to the world. Other people can tell quite a bit about you just from your outer appearance. Are you trendy or retro? Studious or a slacker? An open book or mysterious?

You can become a new person each time you change your clothes. You decide what you want others to see. That guy or girl you were in high school, the one that was a prep, is now a hipster or a geek. Through your appearance, you show what type of people you are most comfortable with and where you fit in on campus.

The Bible has something to say about how you present yourself to the world. As one of God's children, you should clothe yourself in compassion, kindness, humility, gentleness and patience. These traits will draw others to you better than any outfit or new pair of shoes. They will make you more attractive than an expensive haircut or trendy pair of sunglasses ever could.

Today ask God to help you present yourself to the world the way that He sees you and wants you to be seen. Thank Him for reminding us that it is not the clothes we wear but the things we do that make us who we are!

Take My Advice...please

Listen to advice and accept instruction,
that you may gain wisdom in the future.
Proverbs 19:20 ESV

I bet when you were getting ready to leave for college you were inundated with all kinds of advice. Your mom probably gave you tips on laundry and grocery shopping. Your dad probably showed you how to change a tire and balance a checkbook. Grandma might have demonstrated a few karate moves to fend off undesirables and Grandpa finally taught you how to carve a harmonica out of a bar of soap. (Clearly some advice was better than others.)

After awhile, you hear so many different ideas from so many different people that it gets overwhelming. You start to tune some of it out and pretty soon you are tuning all of it out. You give them the wide-eyed, *I'm listening* gaze and combine it with the *really, you don't say?* head nod while you daydream about the day you will be outta this place.

Then you get to college and wish you had listened when mom told you the difference between baking soda and baking powder and explained why you should never put laundry detergent in the dishwasher (even though it is a soap and comes in a box)!

The Bible urges you to listen to advice and to learn new things from other people. None of us knows it all. If someone is nice enough to take the time to teach you something, you should be nice enough to listen to them. You can then decide for yourself what advice to follow or not to follow.

Today ask God to help you be open to listening and learning. Ask Him to put those opportunities in your path so that you may gain wisdom for your future.

The Heavyweight in Your Corner

The LORD your God, who is going before you, will fight for
you, as he did for you in Egypt, before your very eyes.
Deuteronomy 1:30 NIV

The eternal God is your refuge,
and underneath are the everlasting arms.
He will drive out your enemies before you,
saying, 'Destroy them!'
Deuteronomy 33:27 NIV

We often think of God as love. And He is. But He
is many things at many different times. He is our
salvation, our comforter, our provider, our teacher, the
still calm voice that we hear when we are listening. But
God is also our strength and our protector.

The Bible says that the Lord will fight for us, he
will drive out and even destroy our enemies! He is our
champion when we need Him to be. Throughout history,
God's fierceness can be seen in the fall of Jericho, the
plagues of Egypt, the destruction of Sodom and
Gomorrah, the Great Flood. He is truly the Almighty
God!

How wonderful it is to have power like His in your
corner. He is the heavyweight champion of the world,
literally. He will always be the undisputed victor in every
fight and He has *your* back! Today thank the Lord for
His loving and all-powerful protection.

Don't Tempt Me...

No temptation has overtaken you except what is common to mankind. And God is faithful; he will not let you be tempted beyond what you can bear. But when you are tempted, he will also provide a way out so that you can endure it.
1 Corinthians 10:13 ESV

Every day we face temptations to do or say the wrong thing. Usually we overcome these temptations and move on, but every now and then we give in. We tell ourselves we couldn't help it, we couldn't bear it, we just had to do it! But is that really true?

Do you think that you face temptations that no one else has ever faced before? Do you think your temptations are so great that *no one* could overcome them? Do you think that other people have more willpower than you do? That they are stronger or better?

The Bible tells us that every temptation we face is common to mankind. Other people have faced this before and have stayed strong! The Bible tells us that God will not let us be tempted by something that we cannot bear – He will give us the strength to endure it. He will even give us a way out!

The next time you are tempted to do something you know you should not do, take a moment to think. Find those 'exit doors' and plan your escape. God is faithful and He will guide you through and out of the situation if you let Him!

Hey, Good Lookin'

But the LORD said to Samuel, "Do not look on his appearance or on the height of his stature, because I have rejected him. For the LORD sees not as man sees: man looks on the outward appearance, but the LORD looks on the heart." Samuel 16:7 ESV

Bad hair day? Acne? Can't lose that last ten pounds? Fifty pounds? How much time do we put into our appearance each day? We all know people who obsess over their looks. We do it ourselves sometimes and who can blame us? Everything we see on television, in movies and in print tells us to be thinner, fitter, younger-looking and to have whiter teeth and thicker hair. When we don't achieve this ideal of beauty, we tend to feel less lovable, less worthy, just plain unhappy. It is a shame that our looks matter so much.

Think of some of the people that you admire the most, the people that make you laugh, the ones who volunteer to help others, who work in your church, the ones that you want to spend time with because they bring out the best in others. Do you appreciate these people because they are beautiful on the outside or the inside? They might be beautiful people on the surface, but that is not why we want them in our lives. We appreciate the person within. And if we feel this way about others, isn't it fair to say that they feel this way about us? We all know people who get more beautiful the more we get to know them. Others can see us this way as well.

Remember that you are wonderfully made by God, our Father. Let His love and light shine through you and just see how attractive you become to others. Bad hair day? Who cares?!

That's Why They Call It Faith

*Now faith is the substance of things hoped for, the
evidence of things not seen.*
Hebrews 11:1 KJV

It would be so easy to be a true believer if Christ were here with us today. Imagine if He traveled the world giving lectures that we could attend or if He had a nightly cable show that we could watch. We could tell others to check out His latest broadcast or podcast or tweet. It would be easy to follow Him and lead others to Him because we could all see with our own eyes and hear with our own ears how wonderful He is. Maybe we could even meet with Him, speak to Him in person or feel His touch. Wouldn't that be glorious?

I believe that someday we *will* be physically in His presence, but for now we must rely on our faith, the substance of things hoped for and the evidence of things not seen. In our hearts we know what is true. We feel what we cannot see, we believe what we cannot touch, we trust what we cannot know. The Bible guides us in our everyday lives. We can read the words of the apostles and of Jesus Himself. We know the stories to be true and the promises to be fulfilled. We have a deep, abiding and eternal faith in our Lord and Savior.

Today, ask God to help you in your walk of faith. Thank Him for the ability to believe in things unseen and for the hope of the eternal life that He has promised us!

Is There Someone Else I Can Talk To?

But truly God has listened; He has attended to the voice of my prayer. Blessed be God, because he has not rejected my prayer or removed his steadfast love from me!
Psalm 66:19-20 ESV

In the movie, 'Monty Python and the Holy Grail', there is a scene where King Arthur and Sir Galahad are standing at the gates of a French castle yelling up to the guards on the parapet. Arthur is trying to find out if the French have any information about the Holy Grail that he seeks. Instead of answering the questions about the grail, the guards fling insults (and eventually cows, sheep, chickens and ducks!) at them. This abuse goes on for quite awhile. Finally, Sir Galahad asks in a hopeful voice, "Is there someone else up there we can talk to?"

Do you ever have days where you just can't seem to get through to someone? When you have something to say or a feeling to express and no one will listen? It can be so frustrating not being heard! Well, God is always available to listen to you, anytime day or night. He understands your innermost thoughts and feelings and He wants you to come to Him with them. He knows what you are going to say before you say it, but He still wants to hear it. No matter what is happening in your life there is always someone else up there you can talk to and He is waiting to hear from *you!*

Give Thanks in All Circumstances...
really?

...always giving thanks to God the Father for everything,
in the name of our Lord Jesus Christ.
Ephesians 5:20 NIV

I once read an article by a ninety-year old woman who was reflecting on her long life. She was sharing many of the lessons that she had learned over the years. One of the things she said was, "If we all threw our problems in a pile and saw everyone else's, we'd grab ours back!"

The Bible tells us that God wants us to be thankful in good times and in bad. No matter the situation, we should be looking for that silver lining or blessing in disguise. We all have problems and bad days, but we also have so many blessings. Take a minute to count the wonderful things in your life right now. As you think of something, give thanks to God for it. At the end of this gratitude prayer thank God for His greatest gift to us: His son Jesus and the gift of everlasting life.

Be joyful in hope, patient in affliction, faithful in prayer.
Romans 12:12 NIV

According to Your Gifts

Having gifts that differ according to the grace given to us, let us use them: if prophecy, in proportion to our faith; if service, in our serving; the one who teaches, in his teaching;
Romans 12:6-7 ESV

You have a very special talent. No, really, you do. It is a talent that God specifically gave just to you. Maybe your talent is an artistic one like the ability to paint or sing or dance. Maybe it is the ability to organize, problem-solve or get along well with others. Whatever it is, the Bible says that God wants you to use it.

Today, write down all of the things that you do well. No negativity allowed! If you can't come up with anything (surely you can come up with *something*), ask a friend or family member. They will give you a whole list of good stuff! Now look at this list and think about each item; how can you use this to improve your life, the lives of others, and to serve God. Take a moment to thank Him for these talents and to dedicate them to His service. Now go out there and share your gift with the world!

Go Ahead, Ask

And I tell you, ask, and it will be given to you; seek, and you will find; knock, and it will be opened to you.
Luke 11:9 ESV

Whenever I ask God for something that I want, I always finish my prayer with, "Thy will be done". If I don't get what I prayed for I can take comfort in the fact that it isn't God's will for me. This might sound like I have little faith in the power of prayer, but quite the opposite is true. After all, He has promised to take care of all of our needs and to answer our prayers. It's just that sometimes the answer is no or not yet. When I get no for an answer, I can accept it.

How many times have your parents said no when you asked for something that you really wanted but that they felt it would not be good for you? Or maybe they thought that you were not yet old enough or responsible enough to handle it. Maybe they said no because they wanted you to earn the thing for yourself or they wanted you to learn patience. They said no to you out of love and concern. On the other hand, how many times did they say yes to you? And how much sweeter were those moments, knowing that it could have gone either way, but this time you got what you wanted?

God wants you to come to Him. Today, ask for what you really want. Be specific. Ask God to help you find a way to earn it and to use it for His glory. Whatever the outcome, you can trust that your prayer will be heard and answered by your Heavenly Father who has your best interests at heart!

Who Are You?

You have searched me, Lord, and you know me. You know when I sit and when I rise; you perceive my thoughts from afar. You discern my going out and my lying down; you are familiar with all my ways. Before a word is on my tongue, Lord, you know it completely.
Psalm 139:1-4 NIV

For in Christ Jesus you are all children of God, through faith.
Galatians 3:26 NIV

Who are you? At first glance this seems like an easy question to answer: a Christian, a son or daughter, a sibling, a student, a roommate, a team member, a friend. But who are you in God's eyes? Sometimes when we define ourselves, we forget the most important thing. *We are the children of God!* Let that sink in for a moment. The Creator of the entire Universe calls you His own!

Today, take a minute to realize what that truth means to you. As you go through your day keep that thought foremost in your mind. Approach every situation and meet every challenge as a dearly beloved child of the Creator of the Universe. He knows you better than you know yourself and loves you more than humanly possible. That should put a spring in your step!

Yet to all who did receive Him, to those who believed in His name, He gave the right to become children of God.
John 1:12 NIV

17

A New Beginning

In the beginning God created the Heavens and the earth.
Genesis 1:1 ESV

Therefore if any man be in Christ, he is a new creature:
old things are passed away; behold, all things are
become new.
2 Corinthians 5:17 KJV

A new year gives us the opportunity to take inventory of our lives, much like they do in grocery stores and retail centers. They are not only counting the items that they have on hand but planning for the upcoming shopping seasons. What items did not sell very well, which ones flew off the shelves? What do they need more of? What should they discontinue?

Take a quick inventory of your life. Are there things about you that you should "discontinue"? Do you have too much worry, envy, stress, or hopelessness? What about the things that you would like to have more of: time with God or your family, better grades, more friends?

Keep the list you made in your mind and pray about it daily. Be conscious of it at all times and ask yourself, "What did I do today to get closer to obtaining the items on my list?" Take steps every day that will bring you closer to your goals and to God.

Watch Where You Point That Thing

For in the same way you judge others, you will be judged, and with the measure you use, it will be measured to you. Matthew 7:2 NIV

Are we really not supposed to judge others? How can we know who to befriend, pray for, minister to or in some cases avoid if we do not make some sort of preliminary judgments about them? Aren't first impressions a form of judgment? We have and make those all of the time.

I think the key to the above verse is the warning that you will judged with the same measure you use to judge others. In other words, don't be a hypocrite. Before you make that judgment ask yourself: Could I ever end up in his or her situation? If so, how would I behave? Have I ever been *mis*judged because of something that I said or did? And finally, am I truly in the position to pass judgment on another one of God's children?

Obviously we are going to make quick judgments about others based on looks, clothing, mannerisms, speech and the other things that make up that important first impression. But then, take a moment and look again. Try to replace judging with understanding and empathy and you just might find that favor returned to you!

Today ask God to forgive your sins and shortcomings. Ask Him for guidance when dealing with others so that you can become a non-judgmental representative of a loving and forgiving Savior.

A Great Story

And we know that for those who love God all things work together for good, for those who are called according to his purpose. Romans 8:28 ESV

Have you ever noticed that those great stories your grandparents used to tell you were pretty intense? I mean the ones about The War and The Depression, the lack of all the modern conveniences we have today and how they had to survive each and every day with so very little. When we hear these stories today, we have the comfort of knowing how everything turned out. Obviously Grandma lived through this story because she is telling it to us. But back then, Grandma had no idea if she would make it or not.

The real point of these tales is, "Look at what I went through, look how I survived it. Look at the decisions I made and the actions I took that led me to this outcome." They are not stories purely for our amusement, even though they are incredibly entertaining. They are lessons to be learned. They are also comforting because they remind us that people can survive during the toughest of times.

What stories will you pass on to your grandchildren? Will they be happy ones, sad, harrowing, or heartwarming? You are writing your story everyday. Some days are action-packed, some days are mysteries, some days are comedies and some may even be tragedies. But when life is coming at you full speed and you're not quite sure how things are going to turn out, just remember: this will make a great story someday!

Power

*Your right hand, Lord, was majestic in power. Your right
hand, Lord, shattered the enemy.*
Exodus 15:6 NIV

I can do all things through him who strengthens me.
Philippians 4:13 ESV

Have you ever wondered if you have the strength
that is required to do something really hard? Have you
ever tried to quit a bad habit and felt completely
powerless? What about when you have just too much on
your plate with your job, friends and school? What do
we do when faced with something in our lives that
seems impossible to overcome?

What we should do first and foremost is recognize
the obstacle for what it is: an opportunity to succeed, to
accomplish something important, to grow as a person
and as a Christian. We don't have to face these
obstacles alone!

Today, ask God to help you turn your obstacles
into opportunities. The Bible is full of stories about
people facing unimaginable trials and tribulations:
Moses, Joseph, Jonah, and Daniel to name a few. And
God never abandoned not a one of them! He was with
them every step of the way just like He is here for us
today! Parting the Red Sea? Crumbling the walls of
Jericho? Now that is real power! And with power like
that behind you, you can do anything!

Say It Now

A new commandment I give to you, that you love one another: just as I have loved you, you also are to love one another.
John 13:34 ESV

We have all heard the saying, "Treat each day as if it were your last." This is great advice, but what about, "Treat each *person* as if this day were your last,"? Every day we run around in such a hurry that it is easy to overlook the people in our lives. We figure we always have tomorrow to tell them we love them or to give them encouragement. But what if today was your last day? What was the last thing you said to your roommate this morning? Your classmates? Your best friend? Is it something you would be happy to have them remember as your last words to them?

What would you like to tell the people you love today? Would you thank your parents for their unwavering love and support? Or thank your siblings for all of the fun and laughter? Or tell your best friend that you couldn't have made it through the tough times without his or her shoulder to cry on? Whatever it is, you are here right now – so say what you need to say right now, today. And, who knows, you might just hear something nice in return!

Keeping It Positive

Finally, brothers and sisters, whatever is true, whatever is noble, whatever is right, whatever is pure, whatever is lovely, whatever is admirable – if anything is excellent or praiseworthy – think about such things.
Philippians 4:8 NIV

Bless the Lord, O my soul, and forget not all His benefits, who forgives all your iniquity, who heals all your diseases, who redeems your life from the pit, who crowns you with steadfast love and mercy.
Psalm 103:2-4 ESV

Our thoughts can have such an effect on our minds and bodies but we seem to have so little control over them. God wants us to focus on the things that are pure, noble, true, lovely, admirable, excellent and praiseworthy. Psalm 103:2-4 reminds us to "forget not all His benefits".

When we have negative thoughts it creates a toxic atmosphere in our bodies. We can actually make ourselves physically ill or bring on depression. Even worse, we can pass our negativity on to others. Being positive is a decision that we have to make. We can choose what to focus on and what to filter out.

Today if a negative thought crosses your mind immediately replace it with a positive one. Don't let the negative thought have any time at all to take root. Right now, think of several positive situations in your life so that you will be ready with your substitutions. Focus on God and His promises. You can't get any more positive than that!

Rain on My Parade, Please

Rejoice always, pray without ceasing, give thanks in all circumstances; for this is the will of God in Christ Jesus for you.
1 Thessalonians 5:16-18 ESV

Not too long ago, we took a trip to Disneyland. We were so excited for this trip. We planned everything down to the last detail, but we didn't factor in the weather. Well, wouldn't you know, the day we flew into Los Angeles was the last sunny day they would have for a week. Not only was it not sunny, but it rained constantly. We sat in our hotel room looking sadly out the window on that first morning watching our vacation go down the storm drains!

Then we noticed that a few other people were heading for the park. They were all wearing blue rain ponchos purchased from the hotel gift shop. We jumped up, ran downstairs, purchased our ponchos and headed for Disneyland. The place was practically empty except for a few desperate vacationers like us. All of the restaurants and shops were open and so were most of the rides. And the biggest treat of all- no lines for anything! We rode everything twenty times. As soon as we got off of a ride we could turn around and get right back on it if we wanted to. We felt like VIP's who had the place all to ourselves! What a blessing that rain turned out to be for our vacation! When we talk about that trip now no one even remembers being wet (and we were, believe me)!

We don't always know what God has in store for us. A little rain in our lives now and then can turn out to be the biggest blessing! Just put on your big, blue, prayer poncho and go boldly forward!

It's Not Just About You

*In the same way, let your light shine before others,
so that they may see your good works and
give glory to your Father who is in heaven.*
Matthew 5:16 ESV

How many times have you told yourself that you are never going back to a certain restaurant or store because of the treatment that you received from one of their employees? Maybe the restaurant had a great menu and delicious food, but the service was so bad that you couldn't enjoy your dinner. Maybe the store had low prices on high quality items but the salespeople were so rude that you'd rather pay more somewhere else. Sadly, the company representatives are driving the customers away.

When you are out in public, you are a representative as well. You represent your church, your Christian community, the family of God. Are you making a good first impression? After spending time with you, would someone want to 'come back for more'? Would they want to see what makes you the way you are? Would they want to be more like you? Would someone want to know Christ and learn more about being a Christian after spending time with you?

Try to remember this the next time your roommate gets on your nerves, a waiter makes a mistake on your order or is just downright rude to you. Remember it when a stranger asks for help, a friend asks for your time, or your professor springs an unexpected assignment on you. React to the situation in a manner becoming of your very important role – God's representative.

Gear Up

Thy word have I hid in mine heart,
that I might not sin against thee.
Psalm 119:11 KJV

Have you been camping lately? Think about how much thought and preparation goes into a camping trip. You have to plan every meal, plan every activity and have a *back-up* plan for every activity, plan for every type of weather, plan for accidents and unexpected illness. Is there a town close by? An emergency room? What about bears?! You are exhausted before you even leave the house!

But when you get to the campsite and are surrounded by God's beautiful creation you can relax and enjoy your vacation. You realize that you are prepared for almost every situation, expected or not. You have the security that comes from being prepared.

David's Psalm 119:11 is about this same security. He too has 'geared up'. He is ready for challenges and temptations that may arise because he has prepared for them. He has fortified himself and planned for the unexpected, ready to face them when necessary.

Today, think about how you can 'gear up' to face those unexpected twists and turns in your life. Are you prepared for the 'trip' or are you going to be facing that bear with a roll of paper towels and some nail clippers? The choice is up to you.

Increase Your Odds

Commit your work to the Lord,
and your plans will be established.
Proverbs 16:3 ESV

We all know someone who has 'it all'. They seem to have money and time to spare and not a care in the world. They have scholarships, straight 'A's, and popularity. Are we happy for them or do we feel jealous? Do we mope around and say life isn't fair or do we use them as the motivation to improve ourselves?

The Bible says that God wants *us* to be successful, too. He wants to guide and help us in our walk with Him and in our daily lives. He is not going to give us a blank check to fund an extravagant lifestyle, but He *will* honor and bless the hard work that we are willing to invest in our lives.

Persistence creates luck. Today pray for success and for the strength and desire necessary for that success. Then work hard towards your goal. Be persistent and find out just how lucky you really are!

Forgive _And_ Forget

_Be kind to one another, tenderhearted, forgiving
one another, as God in Christ forgave you._
Ephesians 4:32 ESV

_And whenever you stand praying, forgive, if you
have anything against anyone, so that your Father also
who is in heaven may forgive you your trespasses._
Mark 11:25 ESV

Forgiving someone who has wronged us is probably one of the hardest things that we are expected to do. Sure, we can let the little things slide, but the big things, the things that have hurt us deeply emotionally and physically, sometimes just seem unforgivable.

I am reminded of a true story about a woman whose only son was killed by a rival gang member at a party. After a few years, the mother asked to meet her son's killer in prison. During this meeting he apologized for his crime and begged for forgiveness. The mother not only forgave him, but became a regular visitor and advocate for the young man. When he was released from prison she helped him find a place to live – right next door to her. When asked by reporters how she could forgive her son's killer so completely, she gave the credit to God. She also said that forgiving did not diminish the fact that this man killed her son, but it allowed her to move on with her life. The hatred was eating her up inside and she needed to forgive him to heal. As for him, the young man now speaks at schools and prisons, giving God the glory for his salvation and second chance at life. He considers the woman to be the mother he never had.

Do you have someone you need to forgive? Do you wish someone would forgive you for something that you did? Why don't you make today the day that you seek or give that much needed forgiveness? You may change your life-and someone else's-for the better!

Aaah, My Eyes, My Eyes!

I will not look with approval on anything that is
vile. I hate what faithless people do;
I will have no part in it.
Psalm 101:3 NIV

Vampires, werewolves and zombies are all the rage. Everywhere you look there is a book, movie or television series devoted to scaring us silly. We like the excitement that comes from being shocked and frightened by what we see. And a good adrenaline rush every now and then is good for us! It gets our heart racing and our blood flowing. We feel alive with excitement!

But when is it too much – too much gore, violence or terror? As Christians we need to be careful about the things we watch. When we see something, it can't ever be unseen. We know of it now and can recall it whenever we want (or don't want) to. These visions can haunt us and cause us to lose focus on the good things that exist in the world. They can bring us down.

On the other hand, some movies (comedies, romances and adventures) can make us feel happy and content. They are uplifting, exciting and adrenaline-pumping in a good way. Enjoy your scary movie every once in a while if you must, but try to seek out the other stuff, the good stuff, when you are looking for entertainment. Your eyes will thank you!

Today find an uplifting film you haven't seen in a while and invite your roommates to join you on the couch for a good old-fashioned movie night. Thank God for this time that you can spend together laughing!

Sing His Praises!
(Or Hum Along)

Shout with joy to the Lord, all the earth! Worship the Lord with gladness. Come before him, singing with joy.
Psalm 100:1-2 NLT

Let's face it, we are not all gifted with great singing voices. When I sing around the house the dog disappears and the kids start howling and clutching their ears. But even so, when it comes to singing praises, the Bible tells us that God loves to hear our voices. Throughout the Bible there are stories of His people singing and dancing in exultation to the Father with pure, unadulterated praise and joy.

On your way to school today sing praises to the Lord. Find the Christian radio station in your area and tune in or download your favorite Christian album and sing along. Sure, other people might look at you funny, but by the time you reach your destination you will be ready to take on anything. Just keep that song in your heart and hum it all day long!

What's Old is New Again

Therefore if any man be in Christ, he is a new creature:
old things are passed away;
behold, all things are become new.
2 Corinthians 5:17 KJV

The Bible tells us that God doesn't care who we *were*, He cares who we *are*. Isn't that wonderful! No matter what stupid mistakes or bad choices we have made in the past, we are created anew through Christ. When you ask for forgiveness and accept Jesus as your Lord and Savior your sins are washed away forever. He holds no grudges. He harbors no ill feelings. You are His child forever more.

The things of this earth lose their importance. They are just things, after all. The petty vendettas, dramas, and machinations of the human condition slip firmly into the background where they belong. Our focus is now on Him. Our new lives revolve around Him.

Today, rest assuredly in the peace and the promise of the Lord. Take a moment to feel his presence and to experience the pure bliss that overtakes you. You are now ready to have a truly blessed day!

Pushing Forward

*Even there your hand shall lead me and
your right hand shall hold me.
Psalm 139:10 ESV*

Sometimes all we can do is keep putting one foot in front of the other. Our lives get so difficult that we wonder how we can go on. These are the times that we usually find ourselves turning to God and asking for help and guidance. But do we really believe that He will be there to help us? His Word tells us that we can put our trust in Him and expect His help in our toughest times. How wonderful is that?

Think back to a time in your past that was extremely daunting. Knowing what you know now about the outcome of that situation, can you see where God's hand was guiding you? Can you see a lesson that you learned about yourself or others during those times? How did you grow as a person, a friend or a Christian?

Now look at the difficulties you are facing today. Can you imagine how they will look to you five years from now? Can you see what God wants you to gain from today's experiences, how He wants you to grow?

In his kindness God called you to share in his eternal glory by means of Christ Jesus. So after you have suffered a little while, he will restore, support, and strengthen you, and he will place you on a firm foundation. 1 Peter 5:10 NLT

Enemy Mine

But I tell you, love your enemies and
pray for those who persecute you.
Matthew 5:44 NIV

This is a hard one. Are we really supposed to pray for our enemies? For the people who persecute us? The Bible is very clear about this so there must be a reason for it. If we remind ourselves that the people who persecute us are human beings, and not just our adversaries, then we might be able to figure out what makes them tick. Did your tyrannical professor just receive some bad news? Is your snippy roommate having trouble in school? Is that relative you are not speaking to going through a spiritual crisis? Maybe if we prayed for peace and comfort for *them* it would result in peace and comfort for *us* as well.

What if we viewed our "enemies" as people in desperate need of our prayers? If they weren't awful to us, we wouldn't know how much they needed us. The next time you are confronted by one of these people, say a prayer for them, for yourself, and for resolution. You may never be friends with them but hopefully you can improve your relationship and learn to coexist peacefully.

Well, I Didn't Vote for Him

I urge then first of all, that petitions, prayers, intercession and thanksgiving be made for all people— for kings and all those in authority, that we may live peaceful and quiet lives in all godliness and holiness.
1 Timothy 2:1-2 NIV

Now that you are old enough to vote, you get to participate in our country's political system. It is your responsibility to know the issues that affect your country and your community and to pay attention to the candidates and their platforms so that you can make an informed decision on election day. When that day comes, sometimes your candidate wins and sometimes the opposition is victorious. It can be discouraging when someone that does not share your vision for the country or your state becomes the leader of it. What are we to do when we see things changing before our eyes in ways that we feel do not correspond with Biblical teachings?

The Bible tells us to pray for our leaders. We can pray for their health and safety. We can pray for God to guide them as they make the tough decisions that will affect all of our lives. When we have disagreements with them on important issues, we can pray that they have a change of heart or mind. We should not despair, but stay vigilant in our prayers. We should also become politically active and help put the next president into office. Contact your local party chapter and tell them you would like to volunteer. You could distribute campaign literature, answer phones or hang posters around campus. If you don't have time for this, at least make sure you cast your vote on election day. It is not only your right but your responsibility!

There Ain't No Rhyme for Consequences

"A man reaps what he sows."
Galatians 6:7 NIV

What happened to the concept of personal responsibility? Nowadays, if you fail a class, it is the professor's fault. If you can't find a job, it is the government's fault. If you don't get a promotion, it is your manager's fault or a coworkers fault. Once we find someone else to blame we are off the hook. No need to improve or to study or to work harder because someone else is always keeping us down.

Why would we want to give our power away like that? Sure, some things are out of our control, but not everything and certainly not *most* things. If a farmer plants corn he gets a cornfield. If you sow discontent, laziness, apathy, self-pity, blame and bitterness what do you think you will end up with? Who wants to reap that?

What do you want your personal 'bumper crop' to consist of? How hard are you willing to work for it? What do you need in order to plant, nurture and, finally, to reap this crop? Today pray about your future and your goals. Ask God to guide you during your 'growing season' and to bless your efforts with an abundant, spiritually-rich harvest.

Don't Skip to the End

For we live by faith, not by sight.
2 Corinthians 5:7 NIV

There are times when I wish that I could borrow the TARDIS from *Doctor Who* and travel to the future. I would like to see that everything in my life turned out okay. Then I would travel back to this time and enjoy my life knowing that all would be well. When hard times or sickness came upon my family, I could handle it and do what needed to be done without the worry of 'what if'. I could relax and enjoy the little things in life without being constantly caught up in worry about the future.

The problem with this idea, aside from the fact that *The Doctor* would never loan me the TARDIS (and that whole thing about crossing your own time stream), is that it would be just like reading the last page of a book first. I would lose all of the fun of reading the story. There would be no suspense, no surprises, no feeling of accomplishment, no sudden bursts of laughter, no punch lines. I would lose any sense of urgency or motivation. Life, like the book, would be a big yawn.

If we fix our eyes on Christ and walk through this life with Him we will be able to live every moment to the fullest. We don't need to peek ahead to know that everything will turn out for the Glory of God. We need to keep turning the pages of our lives in hopeful anticipation of the adventures that lie ahead!

More Than You Can Handle?

We do not want you to be uninformed, brothers and sisters, about the troubles we experienced in the province of Asia. We were under great pressure, far beyond our ability to endure, so that we despaired of life itself.
2 Corinthians 1:8 NIV

We have all heard that God doesn't give us more than we can handle. Friends have said this to me in times of trouble and I have said it to others who were suffering. I admit that it has helped me through some rough spots, but is this saying always true?

In Psalms 38:4 and 8, David refers to a weight and misery that is far too heavy to bear. In 2 Corinthians 1:8, Paul talks about a pressure far beyond his ability to endure. Maybe things *can* happen to us that we cannot bear after all. So now what? Do we despair? Do we give up?

I think the answer lies in what Paul said in 2 Corinthians 1:9: *Indeed, we felt we had received the sentence of death. But this happened that we might not rely on ourselves but on God, who raises the dead.(NIV)* Paul is saying that sometimes bad things happen to us to bring us closer to God.

Jesus said in Matthew 11:28: *Come to me, all you who are weary and burdened, and I will give you rest. (NIV)*

The Bible promises that God will not fail us nor forsake us (*Deut. 31:6*). While we may face challenges that *we* feel we cannot handle, we will never face *anything* that God cannot handle!

Banana, Anyone?

So God created mankind in his own image,
in the image of God he created them;
male and female he created them.
Genesis 1:27 NIV

All things were made through him, and without him
was not any thing made that was made.
John 1:3 ESV

When you are confronted with the "theory" of evolution in school, remember to think for yourself. Question it the way you would any other unproven theory. For example:

-If we came from monkeys, why are there still monkeys? Shouldn't they all be humans by now?

-One theory says there was a big bang and everything appeared. Isn't that basically what God did? How does this prove that there is no God?

-If we crawled out of a primordial soup and evolved to our surroundings, why didn't we all evolve into the same thing? We had the same surroundings.

-When did we decide to evolve an eyeball? How did we know we needed one? How did we know that there was light and things to see?

-Why did humans evolve an innate need and desire to find God? Since the dawn of time man has sought his creator. Animals don't do that. We have an emptiness that can only be filled by our Lord and Savior.

-How do these theories prove that God does not exist? If anything, they prove that you were wonderfully designed and made by a loving and all-knowing Creator!

Today, thank the Lord for making you in His image and for being in control of our world yesterday, today and tomorrow.

Represent!

*No one has ever seen God; but if we love on another, God
lives in us and His love is made complete in us.*
1 John 4:12 NIV

What does God look like? Does He wear white
robes and sandals? Does He have long white hair and a
flowing, gray beard? Does He look like George Burns or
Morgan Freeman? (Both actors have played Him in
movies, after all.) Is He a bright light shining through
the clouds in perfect, radiant sunbeams?

The Bible says that no one has ever seen God, but
we do have a good 'picture' of Him. If we look at the life
of Jesus, we can see God. If we study Jesus' teachings
and marvel at His miracles, we can see God. If we learn
about the way Jesus treated others when He was here
on earth, we can see God. If we believe the promises
that Jesus gave to us, we can see God. Yes, Jesus is the
best 'picture' that we have of God.

In the same way, we are the best 'picture' that
others have of Jesus. The way we act and speak and
treat others is the only 'picture' many people will ever
see of the Savior. Are you a worthy likeness?

Today, ask the Lord to show Himself to others
through you. Ask Him for guidance as you seek to set a
good example and to share His story with those around
you and thank Him for this awesome opportunity!

One is Silver and the Other is Gold

If either of them falls down, one can help
the other up. But pity anyone who falls
and has no one to help them up.
Ecclesiastes 4:10 NIV

Where would we be without our friends, old and new? We need them to listen to us, comfort us, guide us, laugh and rejoice with us. We feel their love and we send them our love when we are separated from them. We do daring things that we never thought we would and accomplish feats that we never thought we could without the encouragement and backing of our dear friends. We overcome our deepest disappointments and heartaches with their kind understanding and support. We have felt important and needed when we have helped them in return.

God has truly blessed us with the gift of community and companionship. He has charged us with taking care of each other and with loving one another. When we have good friends and are good friends we are sharing His love as well as our own.

Today give thanks for the gift of friendship and for each one of your friends. Pray for their health, well-being and salvation. Now give those friends a call and let them know what you just did. How wonderful to hear that your friend was praying for you!

Now That's A Big S.E.P Field!

Jesus replied, "A man was going down from Jerusalem to Jericho, and he fell among robbers, who stripped him and beat him and departed, leaving him half dead. Now by chance a priest was going down that road, and when he saw him he passed by on the other side. So likewise a Levite, when he came to the place and saw him, passed by on the other side. But a Samaritan, as he journeyed, came to where he was, and when he saw him, he had compassion. He went to him and bound up his wounds, pouring on oil and wine. Then he set him on his own animal and brought him to an inn and took care of him. And the next day he took out two denarii and gave them to the innkeeper, saying, 'Take care of him, and whatever more you spend, I will repay you when I come back.' Which of these three, do you think, proved to be a neighbor to the man who fell among the robbers?" He said, "The one who showed him mercy." And Jesus said to him, "You go, and do likewise."
Luke 10:30-37 ESV

In the novel, "The Hitchhiker's Guide to the Galaxy", there is a phenomenon known as an 'S.E.P. Field'. When this field is surrounding a person or situation requiring attention they are rendered invisible to passers by. The 'S.E.P.' stands for 'Somebody Else's Problem' and it is the most effective shield in the Universe. How many times have we seen and then ignored something or someone that needed our attention or help? Maybe we were in a hurry, or afraid, or just didn't want to get involved.

Jesus told us the story of the Samaritan and his compassion for the injured stranger for a reason. He instructed us to "go and do likewise". Be on the lookout for those in need. Don't let an S.E.P. field obscure your ability to see what is really happening in your home, school, community or in the world around you. Today, pray for guidance as you seek to follow Jesus' instructions regarding those in need.

This Too Shall Pass

And which of you by being anxious can add a
single hour to his span of life?
Matthew 6:27 ESV

As semi-professional worriers (world-class skill, but no pay), we waste a lot of time on things that are beyond our control. We can make ourselves ill or distract ourselves from the tasks at hand. Our pain and suffering will pass. Our trials and tribulations will pass. How we react to them is our choice.

Do we use these hard times as character-building tests to be mightily conquered or do we curl up into the fetal position and let the worry conquer us? Matthew tells us that worrying won't accomplish anything, yet we participate in it far too often. It would be much better for our souls, our health and our psyches to be semi-professional prayer warriors, facing down our worries with the power of the Lord's promises!

We know that we gain nothing, not even one single hour, by worrying. But can we gain something by turning our worries over to God? What about patience, trust, endurance, self-awareness, confidence, a sense of humor? What about a closer relationship to the Lord through our prayers? Maybe there is a reason for our hard times that we could accept and realize - if we just quit worrying about them so much!

What if God Was One of Us?

For I was hungry and you gave me something to eat, I
was thirsty and you gave me something to drink, I was a
stranger and you invited me in, I needed clothes and you
clothed me, I was sick and you looked after me, I was in
prison and you came to visit me.'
Matthew 25: 35-36 NIV

Most of us follow the Golden Rule and treat others the way that we would like to be treated. But do we treat them the way that we would treat Jesus? What *if* God was one of us? According to the Bible verse above, He is. He is your fellow student, your professor and your T.A. He is your roommate, your neighbor and the barrista that makes your latte. He is the homeless man, the hungry child and the stranger on the bus.

What if we treated each person we came across today the way that we would treat Jesus? What if we treated each person we encountered with reverence, respect, honor and love? Could we change their lives a little for the better? Would they pass that love and respect on to others? Could we start a chain-reaction of Christian fellowship and goodwill by gilding our everyday actions with the love of Christ? Wouldn't it be a blessing to find out?

Do not neglect to show hospitality to strangers, for
thereby some have entertained angels unawares.
Hebrews 13:2 ESV

My Body is a What?

*Do you not know that your bodies are temples of the Holy
Spirit, who is in you, whom you have received from God?
You are not your own; you were bought at a price.
Therefore honor God with your bodies.
1 Corinthians 6:19-20 NIV*

Now that you are in complete control of your
health and nutrition you need to make good choices
when it comes to what you eat and drink. You need to
make sure you get enough exercise and that you
practice good hygiene. You owe it to yourself and your
loved ones to keep healthy and fit. Your don't have to be
a super-model or body-builder, but you should take
care of the body that God has given you. How can you
be of service to others if you can't get around? How can
you spend quality time doing what you need to do to
graduate if you can't get up off of the couch?

We control what we put into our bodies and what
we *don't* put into them. A treat every now and then is
nice, but treats shouldn't be a way of life. Resist the
urge to smoke and drink. You have the power to say
'no'.

Make sure to get enough exercise. Pick a friend or
roommate to work out with or to go on walks with. Your
health is precious and as God's beloved creation, you
are worth the effort!

Today thank God for the ability to move and for
the good health that comes with youth. Re-examine
your eating and exercise routines. Are you taking care of
God's temple?

The Words in Red

Jesus answered, "It is written: 'Man shall not live on bread alone, but on every word that comes from the mouth of God.'

Matthew 4:4 NIV

If you look up the above verse in the Bible, you will see that the words Jesus spoke are in red ink. He is talking about the importance of God's Word in our lives even as he is adding to God's Word! He is comparing the Word to the food that we eat. We need both to survive.

I love to flip through my Bible and read the passages highlighted in red because I know these are the words of Jesus, Himself. They are His sermons, parables, instructions, wisdom and insights. They are the actual words of God! What a wonderful feast for my soul!

Take out your Bible, open it to the New Testament and search for the passages in red. Read them aloud, letting them flow from your lips. Feed your soul the daily bread of Christ's teachings and promises. Allow yourself to be completely sated by the words of the Lord!

You Are In Good Hands

*My Father, which gave them me, is greater than all; and
no man is able to pluck them out of my Father's hand.
John 10:29 KJV*

We all like the feeling of belonging. We belong to our families, our friends, our churches and communities and they, in turn, belong to us. But the most important sense of belonging, the one that our souls crave, is the desire to belong to the Lord. The Bible mentions this relationship between God and His children throughout its pages. David sings of it in his psalms!

He holds us in His hands and no one can ever take us away from Him. We can rely on His strength and never-ending devotion. Today, think about your relationship with God. Remind yourself that you belong to Him, the Almighty, the Everlasting. Picture yourself resting in His hands as the world whirls on around you, knowing that you are forever safe and that this is where you truly belong. How wonderful to be able to say, "I am His and He is mine"!

*Blessed assurance, Jesus is mine!
Oh, what a foretaste of glory divine!
Heir of salvation, purchase of God,
Born of His Spirit, washed in His blood.
-Frances J. Crosby, 1873
"Blessed Assurance"*

Unshakeable

Therefore, since we are receiving a kingdom that cannot be shaken, let us be thankful, and so worship God acceptably with reverence and awe,
Hebrews 12:28 NIV

As a Christian, have you ever sat down and really thought about what it is that you are going to inherit from your Heavenly Father? It is something far better than the estates of this earth. It is better than a mansion, a luxury car, a fancy boat or a ton of cash. In fact, the words 'far better than' don't even begin to cover it.

As a child of God, you are the heir to the kingdom of Heaven. You will receive an everlasting life! You will spend eternity in the presence of the Lord! You will have a new body, one that is perfect! You will *never* again experience heartbreak, pain, or sorrow! You will walk streets of gold and sing the Lord's praises for eternity! Your inheritance is 'a kingdom that cannot be shaken'!

Today, think about the true awesomeness of your heavenly inheritance. Give God the awe-inspired thankfulness that this gift, the greatest of all inheritances, deserves!

Weakness to Strength

*But he said to me, "My grace is sufficient for you, for my
power is made perfect in weakness." Therefore I will
boast all the more gladly of my weaknesses, so that the
power of Christ may rest upon me.*
2 Corinthians 12:9 ESV

Most of us do not boast about our weaknesses.
We like to keep those to ourselves as much as possible.
Sometimes they are obvious to others no matter what
we do to keep them hidden. Sometimes, no matter how
hard we try, we just cannot turn them into strengths.
They remind us that we are imperfect beings in an
imperfect world. But is that *all* bad?

The Apostle Paul tells us that the Lord's grace is
with us in our imperfections. His power is made perfect
in our weaknesses and His grace is sufficient for our
shortcomings. The more imperfect we are, the more
perfect the Lord's power becomes in us.

Paul said he would gladly boast of his
imperfections. I am not sure that I would go that far,
but I get what he is trying to say. And I believe it. I will
strive to work on my imperfections and to improve on
the things that I can, but I will not wallow in the ones
that I cannot change. I will accept God's grace and
perfect power for those!

Asking With Confidence

*Let us then with confidence draw near to
the throne of grace, that we may receive mercy
and find grace to help in time of need.*
Hebrews 4:16 ESV

It can be so hard to ask for help sometimes. We feel that there is a weakness in it. Most of us were taught to pull ourselves up by our own bootstraps and to take care of other people in their time of need.

But we can all find ourselves in times of trouble, times when we need emotional, spiritual or physical help. The Bible tells us to ask for God's mercy and grace when we need it. Not only does it tell us to ask, it tells us to ask with *confidence.* It doesn't sound like asking for help is something to be ashamed of, does it?

It is good to use the ole bootstraps to pull yourself up *most* of the time. It builds character and it is good for your soul. You can help others more easily if you can take care of yourself. But there is no shame in falling on hard times and when we need Him, He is there, ready to bestow upon us His mercy and His grace.

Good and Plenty

You have multiplied, O Lord my God,
your wondrous deeds and your thoughts toward us;
none can compare with you!
I will proclaim and tell of them,
yet they are more than can be told.
Psalm 40:5 ESV

God is so generous with us. Have you ever tried to put down on paper all of the wonderful blessings that he has bestowed upon you? The words would just flow onto the page. Your list would go on and on. At some point, you might find yourself, like David, not able to name them all. *"I will proclaim and tell of them, yet they are more than can be told."*

And it is not just the sheer number of blessings that we have received, it is the size and scope of them that is so awe inspiring. It is the patience and guidance that comes with them. It is the deep and unending love with which those gifts were given to us. David praises God for His wondrous deeds *and thoughts* toward us. The Lord gives us his *attention* as well as His deeds. I think this is one of the best blessings of all!

Today, proclaim God's wondrous deeds in your life. Share them with a friend, roommate, or classmate. Write them down, reflect on them and thank the Lord for each one.

Restoration for the Weary

He renews my strength. He guides me along right paths,
bringing honor to his name.
Psalm 23:3 NLT

He restoreth my soul: he leadeth me in the paths of
righteousness for his name's sake.
Psalm 23:3 KJV

When my daughter was in college she worked part-time in a coffee shop. She was amazed at how the most obnoxious customers could turn into the nicest people after they had taken their first sip of coffee. How did these ogres turn into teddy bears so quickly? We all know the answer to that one – caffeine-induced bliss!

We all need a pick-me-up now and then. Sometimes it is a physical pick-me-up. Sometimes it is mental or emotional. But what about a spiritual one? The Bible tells us that God is with us always. He can provide rest and *restoration* for the weary soul. In Psalms, David sings of the Lord renewing his strength and then guiding him along the right paths, the paths of righteousness.

So, go ahead and have that java jolt when your body needs a kick start, but remember to rely on God when you need true strength and restoration. Start your day with a grande sized cup of glory and a venti 'Halleluia' – then go get your coffee!

Faith Like a River

Here is a saying you can trust.

If we died with him,
we will also live with him.
If we don't give up,
we will also rule with him.
If we say we don't know him,
he will also say he doesn't know us.
Even if we are not faithful,
he will remain faithful.
He must be true to himself.

2 Timothy 2:10-13 NIV

What did Timothy mean when he said that God must be true to Himself? That even if we are not faithful, He will be? I think he was telling us that God is constant. He is who He says He is. He is unchanging, unwavering, strength upon strength, true and faithful. No matter what we do, or don't do, it will not change Him. Our moods and emotions can be ever changing, but the Lord is not.

He has made promises to us and we can rest assured that He will keep them. He has left us His Word to guide us. He surrounds us with His love and protection and we know that we will always have both. We can know and trust these things because He says we can – and he is always faithful, even if we are not.

Today, read the above verse and think about its meaning. God will keep the promises stated in it. Will you keep to your side of the agreement? Will you be a faithful follower worthy of the Lord's faithfulness to you?

The Future's So Bright
I Have to Wear Shades

For I know the plans I have for you," declares the LORD,
"plans to prosper you and not to harm you, plans to give
you hope and a future.
Jeremiah 29:11 NIV

When you think about your future, how far in advance do you go? Next week, five years from now, twenty? What about eternity? Your life after this life? As a Christian you have been promised a glorious life everlasting, a life in the presence of and in fellowship with our Lord. It is a life with no sin, no suffering, no pettiness, no greed, no pain.

Sometimes you can get so bogged down in your day-to-day earthly existence. The future seems so far from now. You might lay in bed at night and wonder what will become of you. Will you pass the test, will you graduate, will you get a good job? You might worry about the direction our country is headed or about the world around us. In the above verse, God tells us that he has plans for each of us, plans of hope and prosperity.

While you do need to consider your situation and make plans of action to improve your life, you should allow yourself to be comforted by the wonderful future that awaits all of God's children. Work hard, persevere, strive for excellence in all things and focus on the glorious future that God has planned for you here on earth and in Heaven!

You Catch More Unicorns With Rainbows

Gracious words are a honeycomb,
sweet to the soul and healing to the bones.
Proverbs 16:24 NIV

I never really liked the phrase, "You catch more flies with honey." It just didn't seem very motivational. I mean, who wants to have a bunch of flies around? But the message is a good one. It is much better to approach others with kindness if you want them to listen to you. Anger and frustration will just drive them away.

We can have the best of intentions, but if we do not have the gracious words or calm voice to go with them we can relay the wrong message. It is not always what we say, but how we say it. We must choose our words carefully and think before we speak. The next time you have a confrontation with someone, take a breath, a heartbeat, to think about the words you are about to say. Can you turn the vinegar into honey? Proverbs tells us that gracious words are sweet and healing. And besides, they go down a lot easier if you have to eat them later!

Promises, Promises

Blessed be the LORD who has given rest to his people Israel, according to all that he promised. Not one word has failed of all his good promise, which he spoke by Moses his servant.   *1 Kings 8:56 ESV*

We have all made promises that we did not keep. Sure, we had the best of intentions when we made them, but things happened that got in the way. We apologized for our broken promises, were forgiven and moved on, determined to do better next time. We are only human, after all.

The Lord has made many promises to us. But can you think of one promise He has not kept? I know your life isn't perfect and you have troubles like everyone else, but He never promised us smooth sailing or life on Easy Street. What He did promise was that He would give us comfort and strength in times of trouble. He will give our weary souls rest. He will guide our paths to righteousness. He will love us eternally. He will go and prepare a place for us in Heaven. These are important promises that He keeps and has *always* kept.

Today, thank the Lord for the eternal promises He has made to you. Ask for His guidance in keeping your promises. Is there one that you have not fulfilled yet? Maybe today is the day to keep a promise of your own.

It's a Marathon, Not a Sprint

Do you not know that in a race all the runners run, but only one receives the prize? So run that you may obtain it. Every athlete exercises self-control in all things. They do it to receive a perishable wreath, but we an imperishable.
1 Corinthians 9:24-25 ESV

Competitors do not enter contests intending to lose them. They want to win the prize, whatever it may be. The above verse refers to a race where the prize was a wreath, but it really could have been anything. Winning was the goal and the wreath represented the win.

The athlete had to train hard and exercise self-control. They had to watch what they ate and drank, how much they slept, how much they exercised. They had to constantly think of their goal and consistently strive to get it. The prize was everything to the racer...that all-important, perishable wreath.

Paul was telling the Corinthians to think of their Christianity as a footrace. Focus on the race as though only one person can win. Put as much effort and thought into it as any serious athlete would. And the prize? Not some earthly token that will fall to dust someday, but something *imperishable*, something invaluable, a trophy like no other!

Pray for guidance as you run your life's marathon. Ask for the concentration, determination and focus of a seasoned athlete to help you through today and every day going forward.

Enough Said

I am Alpha and Omega, the beginning and the ending,
saith the Lord, which is and which was, and which is to
come, the Almighty.
Revelation 1:8 KJV

There are so many things written and said about God and religion. There are so many opinions, theories and explanations, books, movies and television shows, songs, paintings, sculptures, mini-series and on and on. I have my thoughts and opinions, you have yours. We were raised in different households, we had different families, different traditions. We are bombarded by so much information, true and untrue, that we can start to question our faith or the faith of others. What do we do when this happens?

I like to get back to basics when things get overwhelming. What do I know to be true and how do I know it? The Bible is God's Word. I can believe what is in it. I can read the words of Jesus Himself. I can read the words of the apostles and the prophets. I don't need outside influences to tell me what God wants me to know. I can read it for myself.

God said, "I am the Alpha and Omega, the beginning and the ending...." and that is good enough for me!

The Past Has Passed

Forget the former things; do not dwell on the past. See, I am doing a new thing! Now it springs up; do you not perceive it? I am making a way in the desert and streams in the wasteland.
Isaiah 43:18-19 NIV

How many times have we been told to let the past go? How many times have we actually done it? It is easier said than done. But we have to move on from the things of the past, we have to enjoy the blessings of those days, live through the trials, learn those lessons, and then move on to the next phase. If we don't, we keep the door closed on the experiences to come and we deny ourselves the knowledge and wisdom that come with them.

I love the mental picture I get when I read the above verse. I see a vast wasteland. Nothing there but rocks and sand. Then, suddenly, a river comes flowing up through the earth, spreading water and life as it makes it way through the desolation. Plants and animals spring up all around. A beautiful oasis is created where there was nothing. Something *new* where there was only desert.

Forget the former things; do not dwell on the past. Let bygones be bygones and step forward. Create something new and watch as your own future springs forth!

God Is Good

*The Lord is good, a stronghold in the day
of trouble; and He knoweth them that trust in Him.
Nahum 1:7 KJV*

The Lord is good - simple and yet so profound. He is the goodness all around us. He is the kindness shared with us and that we share with others. He is the calming touch, the gentle words of comfort, encouragement and praise. He is the good deed, the selfless act, the hope of the discouraged, the best of intentions.

There is no gray area with God. He is completely, utterly, totally, always and in all things genuinely *good*! Think about what the above verse means to you. Your God, who is infinitely good, knows you. He doesn't just know who you are – he knows *you*!

Let God's goodness flow through you today. Try to internalize it and express it in all that you do. And if someone wishes you a 'good day', you can emphatically say, "Yes, it is!"

The Best Medicine

*Then our mouth was filled with laughter, and our tongue
with shouts of joy; then they said among the nations,
"The Lord has done great things for them."
Psalm 126:2 ESV*

When was the last time you had a good old-fashioned belly laugh? Remember how great you felt afterward? Laughter is called the best medicine because it is hard to find something that makes us feel better emotionally and physically. We love the carefree, exhilarating, emotional high that laughter gives us. So why don't we do it every day?

Life doesn't always give us cause for laughter. Some days are just too busy or stressful to even think about laughing. Sometimes its hard to find something to make us crack a smile, let alone laugh out loud. These humor-less stretches in our lives call for action!

Try to look for the 'funny' that is all around you. Let's face it, some of those stressful things that happen at school or work can be quite hilarious if you step back and view them from another angle. Think about how you will tell this "funny" story to your roommates later. Turn it into a comedy! It's all in your attitude!

Smile even if you don't feel like it. Soon you will! Make other people laugh and you will, too. God wants us to be happy and to laugh out loud. After all, we were made in God's image and he definitely has a sense of humor – Platypus, anyone?

When In Doubt, Pray It Out

If you abide in me, and my words abide in you, ask whatever you wish, and it will be done for you.
John 15:7 ESV

Therefore I tell you, whatever you ask in prayer, believe that you have received it, and it will be yours.
Mark 11:24 ESV

When in doubt, pray it out. Go to the Lord and speak your problems and concerns aloud to Him. Make your requests of Him and tell Him your fears. Lay it all out before Him, hiding nothing and holding nothing back.

Pray with confidence and courage. Pray with humbleness and gratitude. Make time for and spend time with your Heavenly Father. Feel the presence of the Holy Spirit all around you. Accept His love and give yours in return. Bask in His glory. Experience the wonder that is inherent in a deep and meaningful relationship with your creator and savior.

Abide in the Lord and let His words abide in you, believe that your prayers will be answered, have faith and it will all be done for you. The above verses are 'the words in red', the words of Jesus Christ, Himself!

Today experience the gifts of faith and spirit that were promised to you through prayer. What a glorious way to start your day!

Read It Again… For the First Time

The LORD is my shepherd; I shall not want. He maketh me to lie down in green pastures: he leadeth me beside the still waters. He restoreth my soul: he leadeth me in the paths of righteousness for his name's sake. Yea, though I walk through the valley of the shadow of death, I will fear no evil: for thou art with me; thy rod and thy staff they comfort me. Thou preparest a table before me in the presence of mine enemies: thou anointest my head with oil; my cup runneth over. Surely goodness and mercy shall follow me all the days of my life: and I will dwell in the house of the LORD for ever.
Psalm 23:1-6 KJV

Today I invite you to read Psalm 23:1-6 as though you were reading it for the first time. Really think about what David is saying, enjoy the prose and poetry, appreciate the artistry of his song and contemplate the meaning of his words. Our cups truly *do* runneth over and goodness and mercy *shall* follow us all the days of our lives. Hallelujah!

Thank the Lord today for the personal relationship that you share with Him. Thank Him for walking with you through this life and the next. Praise His holy name!

Keep Moving Heavenward

"Brothers, I do not consider myself yet to have taken hold of it. But one thing I do: Forgetting what is behind and straining toward what is ahead, I press on toward the goal to win the prize for which God has called me heavenward in Christ Jesus."
Philippians 3:13-14 NIV

Every day we are moving in one direction or another. Some days we make a lot of progress towards the completion of our many tasks and goals. Other days we take two steps forward and one step back. Things pop up unexpectedly causing us to change course or drop plans altogether. Once we have taken care of these bumps in the road we can get back on track and start moving forward again.

In our spiritual lives it is important to make forward progress as well. In Philippians, Paul talks about forgetting the past and straining towards a goal, a prize. He acknowledges that he is not yet where he needs to be. None of us are. But the journey to get there is important. We must pray, study the Bible, have fellowship with other Christians and share the good news of the Lord with others.

What will you do today to progress in your spiritual journey? Will you make time for Bible study, self-reflection and prayer, assist someone less fortunate, or call on a sick friend? Strive to achieve your spiritual goals as hard as you do your earthly ones. Keep moving Heavenward towards the *ultimate* goal.

Make the Commitment

Commit thy way unto the LORD;
trust also in him; and he shall bring it to pass.
Psalm 37:5 KJV

Let's face it, some of us are just better at making commitments than others. Some people look at a commitment as something they'll try to get to. No big deal. But others take their commitments seriously. They would walk ten miles barefoot in a blizzard to do the thing that they committed to do!

You make commitments all of the time. You commit to showing up to work and doing the tasks for which you were hired. You commit to your professors that you will listen and participate in class. You commit to doing your homework. You commit to your parents that you will be responsible and will study hard. But what about making a commitment to the Lord?

David is telling us that if we commit our lives, our hearts and our purpose to the will of the Lord and we trust completely in Him, He will commit to us in return. He will bring about the desires of our soul and help us reach our goal of closeness to Him.

Have you made a true commitment to Jesus? If not, take the time to think about what that would mean to you. Are you ready for a full and meaningful relationship with Christ? If you are unsure, pray for guidance or seek council from your clergy or youth group leader. And when you are ready, make that commitment wholeheartedly and seriously. This is a commitment that is not always easy, but is always worth it. This a commitment worth keeping!

Make Your Words Count

So shall my word be that goeth forth out of my mouth: it shall not return unto me void, but it shall accomplish that which I please, and it shall prosper in the thing whereto I sent it.
Isaiah 55:11 KJV

Words are so powerful. We can use them to heal aching hearts, calm nerves, encourage others, tell a funny or uplifting story, express love, ask for help, convey knowledge, and most importantly, share the gospel of our Lord with others.

Words can be weapons as well. They can wound, crush, bury and sting. We can intentionally and even unknowingly cause so much harm with the words that we say. With such a powerful arsenal at our disposal, you would think that we would have to have a license to speak at all!

Today, think about your words before you say them. Let everything that you say be uplifting, encouraging and thoughtful. Say what you mean and mean what you say. Give the gift of gab the gravitas that it deserves. Don't be frivolous or petty or cruel with your words, send them out to 'prosper' wherever they go. Ask God to guide your words today and to help you think before you speak.

Praise Ye The Lord, Hallelujah

O praise the LORD, all ye nations: praise Him, all ye people. For His merciful kindness is great toward us: and the truth of the LORD endureth for ever.
Praise ye the LORD.
Psalm 117:1-2 KJV

Make today a day of praise. Make everything you do today glorify God. If you have school work to do today, do it with a cheerful and grateful spirit. Praise God for this wonderful opportunity to use your gifts and your mind and ask Him to bless these endeavors.

If you are playing today, praise God for His beautiful world and the gift of fun! Enjoy your recreation to the fullest, expressing gratitude that our creator has blessed us with laughter, friendships and joyful times.

If you are ill or grieving or lonely, praise God that these times will pass. Praise Him for the gift of hope that helps to lift us out of these low times. Praise Him for the life that we will live with Him in Heaven, where there is no sickness or death and where we will be reunited with our loved ones.

Whatever you are doing, wherever you are, praise Him with all of your heart today. And everyday. As David sang, 'O praise the Lord, all ye nations: praise Him all ye people....'"

God As Man

Jesus wept.
John 11:35 KJV

Remember all of the WWJD merchandise that was so popular a few years ago? 'What would Jesus do?' was trendy but it was also a good way to think about the decisions that we make. What *would* Jesus do in this situation or that one?

When we remember that Jesus was a man, a human being like the rest of us, it gives new meaning to the question. He lived here on earth with us and as one of us. He had emotional and physical needs, human thoughts, a flesh-and-blood body. It is an honest query – what would He do or think about this or that?

If you want to know Jesus, read the New Testament. Follow His story and learn about how he treated others, those above and below His earthly station, the sick, the rich, the poor, the powerful, the weak. Read the sermons He gave and the lessons He imparted to His disciples and the crowds that followed Him. Read how He faced His death with courage and conviction, but also with very human feelings like fear and sadness. Read how He triumphed over death and this earthly realm so that we could do it as well. When you are finished you will have a good idea of what Jesus would do and a good idea of what you should do as well.

Today thank God for sending His son to live as one of us. Thank Him that we can use Jesus' example in living our own lives here on this earthly plain. WWJD? Let's find out!

Mountain Strong

They that trust in the LORD shall be as mount Zion,
which cannot be removed, but abideth for ever.
Psalm 125:1 KJV

I have never been a physically strong person. I was an uncoordinated, gangly kid that galloped through P.E. trying not to fall flat on my face. I trip on my own feet, I walk into walls, I need someone to open jars for me and carry the vacuum cleaner upstairs. Not a paragon of strength by any means am I.

But as a Christian, I can be as strong as a mountain. I like to imagine myself as steadfast and powerful, able to withstand the wind and weather, the tide and the times. A mountain that abideth forever and cannot be removed.

We can gain strength when we need it by realizing that we already possess it. We, that trust in the Lord, are strong. We know that we cannot be beaten down, we cannot be moved or broken. We know what we stand for and we know what we would die for. We know where we are going to spend our eternity. The things of this earth cannot truly hurt us for we can bear all with the strength and power that our trust in God gives us.

Today, thank God for His gift of strength. Remember that you are mountain strong and can do all things through Him!

The Foundation's The Thing

Unless the LORD builds the house,
the builders labor in vain.
Unless the LORD watches over the city,
the guards stand watch in vain.
Psalm 127:1 NIV

We humans think that we can do it all. In fact, we can get downright cocky about it. If we can dream it up, we can do it. And we *have* done some pretty incredible things, things that our ancestors probably never even imagined.

We can fly around the globe, we can go to the moon, we build skyscrapers miles high and then, just because we can, we put roller coasters on top of them (really, I saw this on YouTube!)! We engage in commerce and politics on a global scale. We establish worldwide charities and humanitarian efforts and the list goes on and on. We *are* pretty cool when you think about it.

But what does it all mean? Are all of these feats done for the glory of God or the glory of man? David said that no matter how much we build or do, it is all in vain unless the Lord is involved. We need to remember to include Him in our endeavors, to pray for guidance and wisdom as we 'build our skyscrapers'. We need to remember that He is our rock and foundation and that what is built on Him will not be built in vain.

Today, include God in all that you do. Keep Him in mind as you make decisions, big and small. Ask Him to guide and support in your work and play. He is the master builder, after all.

Listen Carefully

Your own ears will hear him.
Right behind you a voice will say,
"This is the way you should go,"
whether to the right or to the left.
Isaiah 30:21 NLT

We have all experienced intuition in one form or another. Sometimes it is a chill up your spine or a tingling in your gut. You feel that something is not right and you change your course or your plans. Sometimes you ignore these feelings and when you think back on them you wish you had listened to what they were trying to tell you.

We write songs about listening to our hearts and following our dreams. We are told by our elders to trust our gut feelings. What does this mean? Do we possess powers that we are not aware of? Are we psychics tapping into the power of the universe, as our secular friends like to believe? Should we buy crystals and incense and start meditating?

The answer is that we *are* spiritual beings. We have been divinely created by our loving and ever-present God. We are connected to Him through the sacrifice of His son, Jesus Christ. We can feel His presence through the Holy Spirit and if we listen hard enough, we can hear that still, small voice telling us which way to go. Crystals are for those poor souls still desperately seeking that which is so easy to find. The answer that is right in front of them: the love of their Heavenly Father.

Today, thank God for His presence in your life. Thank Him for His wisdom and guidance. Ask Him to help you listen for His voice above all of the cacophonic noises of the world. Then be still and listen.

Don't Forget the Guidebook

Thy word have I hid in mine heart,
that I might not sin against thee.
Psalm 119:11 KJV

The last time we went on a vacation I really did my research. I found out all I could about our destination. I researched and compared hotels. I read blogs about things to do while we were there. I read reviews on restaurants and coffee shops. After all, we don't go on vacation that often and we wanted it to be as perfect as possible.

I went to the bookstore and found that there are guidebooks written about almost every place in the world. There is even a *Hitchhiker's Guide to the Galaxy*, but I don't need one of those...yet. It was amazing all of the things I could learn about a destination in one convenient, leather-bound book. It made traveling a breeze and we had a wonderful time!

We Christians have a guidebook as well. It was commissioned by our Heavenly Father, inspired by His love for us and written by His followers. It is the guidebook for His children. A place where we can find the answers to our questions, comfort in times of trouble, hope in the face of despair, stories to inspire us and teach us, examples that we can follow and so much more.

Do you keep your guidebook handy? Is your Bible on your nightstand, on your desk or maybe even in your car? Today, find your Bible and put it within reach so that you can refer to it every day. Take it out and really get to know it. Learn the books of the Bible. Find out who the author of each book is and learn something about them. Read the index and the footnotes. Get a Study Bible or just study the one you have. This is your guide – don't get caught without it.

Do Not Despair

"I have told you these things, so that in me you may have peace. In this world you will have trouble. But take heart! I have overcome the world."
John 16:33 NIV

The LORD is close to the brokenhearted and saves those who are crushed in spirit.
Psalm 34:18 NIV

Most of us have suffered grief in our lives. We are mortal beings who must all leave this earth some day. Some of us live many years and some of us make just a brief appearance here on earth. Many who live those short lives make bigger impacts on the world around them than some who live long, long lives. And almost everyone leaves behind someone who loves them, someone who is devastated by their passing. When we are the ones left behind, it can be hard to make sense of our loss. We feel that no one else can understand our grief. We feel that God is very far away. Sometimes we are mad at God for not giving us more time with our loved one. We wonder where He was when we needed Him the most. We look around us and wonder how the world can still go on in the face of our loss.

The Bible tells us that the Lord is close to the brokenhearted. He is always with us. Do not let your grief keep you from reaching out to Him. We will all experience death and the excruciating pain of loss. It is part of our imperfect and sinful world. But we will have victory over death. We will see our loved ones again. We are the hopeful, beloved children of God, and we will all be together again in Heaven.

Today pray for someone you know who is suffering. Ask God to make His presence known to them and to comfort them. Reach out to them yourself and let them know that you are praying for them and that you have not forgotten them or their lost loved one. You might even be an answer to *their* prayers for comfort and assurance. Let the Lord use you today.

Teach Me to Pray

After this manner therefore pray ye:
Our Father which art in heaven, Hallowed be thy name.
Thy kingdom come. Thy will be done in earth, as it is in
heaven. Give us this day our daily bread. And forgive us
our debts, as we forgive our debtors. And lead us not into
temptation, but deliver us from evil: For thine is the
kingdom, and the power, and the glory, for ever. Amen.
Matthew 6: 9-13 KJV

Jesus Himself taught us how to pray. He gave us an example to follow. When we pray, we should remember to acknowledge God as our Father, we should praise His name, we should acknowledge that it is His will and not our own that we seek. We should approach Him with the reverence and respect that He deserves.

We should ask God to provide for our physical and spiritual needs, our daily bread. All good things come from Him and we know this. We must ask Him for forgiveness, for we are sinful beings, but if we seek forgiveness for ourselves, we must also be ready to give it to others.

Jesus knew that every day is a struggle. We are faced with temptations and we must chose to stay on the right path. He knew that we would need God's help to deliver us from the evil that we come up against in our daily lives. We are not perfect, but He is.

And finally, we should close our prayers with the acknowledgement of God's never-ending power and glory. Does God need to hear this from us? No, but *we* need to hear it to remind us to whom we are praying.

Today, pray the Lord's prayer. Think of each line as you say it. Glory in these word's that came from Jesus Himself. Remember to use this template when praying your own prayers in the future. His is the kingdom, and the power, and the glory, forever!

Love Bigger Than Yourself

If a man say, "I love God," and hateth his brother, he is a liar. For he that loveth not his brother whom he hath seen, how can he love God whom he hath not seen?
John 4:20 KJV

There are so many verses in the Bible about loving your neighbor, caring for strangers, and not judging others unless you want to be judged yourself. The above verse tells us not to hate anyone and if we do then we cannot love God. Why all this instruction regarding those around us?

God is our Father, our creator. He loves each of us in the same way. He loves us equally. He loves the murderer on death row as much as He loves the pastor delivering sermons to His people every Sunday. His love knows no bounds.

As His children and His representatives here on earth, God wants us to love and care for one another. He wants us to love the saved and the sinner alike. After all, if He can love us, with all of our inadequacies, imperfections, and sinfulness, who are we to deny this of our brothers and sisters? Yes, some people are definitely easier to love than others, but we must make the effort when necessary. There are times when *we* are hard to love as well.

Today ask God to help you love your fellow man, not just tolerate him. We have our limitations, but He does not. Ask Him to fill your heart with His love so that you may share it. Ask Him to help you love beyond your capacity, to love bigger than yourself!

The Support Team Could Use Some Support

I urge you, brothers and sisters, by our Lord Jesus Christ and by the love of the Spirit, to join me in my struggle by praying to God for me.
Romans 15:30 NIV

The writers of the New Testament prayed for the new Christian churches forming around them and they also asked for prayer in return. They needed the blessings that come from the prayer of others just as much as the new believers did.

We sometimes forget that our spiritual leaders are human beings like us. They have the same needs that we do. They suffer the same struggles and stresses as well. On top of that, they have the added responsibility of guiding and nurturing a congregation and the individuals who make up that congregation. They were called to ministry and they accepted the call knowing that they would lead a blessed life, but not an easy one.

Today, pray for your clergy, locally, nationally and internationally. Include our many missionaries in this prayer. Thank God for their sacrifices and commitment to His church. Ask Him to bless and guide them in their daily work and to cloak them in the protection of the Holy Spirit. After you have prayed for them think of something supportive that you could do for them. Maybe you could bring them a cup of coffee or a meal, volunteer for youth group or write them note letting them know how much you appreciate them. How lovely it is to take care of those who take care of us!

Random Acts

And be ye kind one to another...
Ephesians 4:32 KJV

Earlier I mentioned that my daughter worked at a coffee house where she had a front row seat to the pre- and post-caffeinated moods of humanity. She also was witness to some random acts of kindness and their effects on others.

Every now and then a customer would pull through the drive-thru window and pay for their coffee as well as the coffee of the customer in the car behind them. That person would then pull up to the window and be pleasantly surprised with a free drink courtesy of a complete stranger. Sometimes it would end there with the two happy and blessed strangers. But sometimes the kindness would keep going and going with each new customer. Upon finding that their drink was purchased for them they would pass the kindness on and buy for the next person in line. This could go on for hours! (Usually ending when a car containing one passenger was followed by a car containing six. Completely understandable.)

During these pay-it-forward buying sprees the whole restaurant would get caught up in the action. The baristas and lobby customers would realize what was happening in the drive-thru and a general buzz of happiness and excitement would occur throughout the place. *Everyone* loves a good old-fashioned random act of kindness!

Today, commit an act of kindness of your own. This doesn't have to involve money, just do something nice. You never know what you might start or how many people you might effect. You could be the one good thing that happens to someone today. Wouldn't that be a blessing?

Us vs. Them

Have nothing to do with foolish, ignorant controversies;
you know that they breed quarrels. And the Lord's
servant must not be quarrelsome but kind to everyone,
able to teach, patiently enduring evil, correcting his
opponents with gentleness. God may perhaps grant them
repentance leading to a knowledge of the truth,
2 Timothy 2:23-25 ESV

We all know the two subjects that you should never bring up at a party: politics and religion. Have you ever wondered why these two topics of conversation can lead to such discourse and discomfort in a group of friends or family? Why don't the people we know best just believe the way we do? How do we bring them around to our side without alienating them or causing discourse in our relationships?

We all have our own life experiences that shape our belief systems. No one has lived the exact same life as anyone else. Even children from the same family grow up differently based on their birth order and what the family's social and financial situations were when they were growing up. Not to mention that we are all born with different personality traits, strengths and weaknesses. It's a wonder we can agree on anything at all.

We are emotional as well as physical beings who sometimes base our belief systems on our feelings. We all know a person who is passionate about a certain political candidate or issue but can't tell you why. They just *feel* it.

Therefore, if you must bring up religion or politics, and sometimes it *is* necessary, make sure you have done your homework. Know both sides of an issue, not just the talking-points of one side. Present your case calmly and respectfully. Let the other person respond. Be sincere but not pushy and know when to back off. You don't need to grow an orchard, just plant a seed. Then nurture it with respect, love and prayer and see what comes up.

Keep Calm and Carry On

...and to make it your ambition to lead a quiet life: You should mind your own business and work with your hands, just as we told you, so that your daily life may win the respect of outsiders and so that you will not be dependent on anybody.
1 Thessalonians 4:11-12 NIV

Do you want to have a happy and peaceful life? I think we would all say 'yes' to that question, but how do we achieve this elusive goal? The Bible gives us the blueprint for this life in the above verse: mind your own business, work hard, do not be dependent on anyone else, earn the respect of others.

Minding our own business does not mean that we turn a blind eye to suffering or that we ignore those around us. It just means that we should avoid the petty dramas that come up now and then. Stay away from the campus gossip. Don't be the campus gossip. Don't insert yourself into the personal business of others. Focus on your own relationships, work and goals. Make sure your own life is in order.

When we work, or study so that we can work later on, we create something that we can be proud of. We have a place to focus our thoughts and energy. Idle hands *are* the devil's playground. We have all seen stories on the news of the high crime rates in cities and neighborhoods where there are no jobs. People on welfare sit on stoops and dream of a better day when they were able to work for a living. They have lost their zest for life.

When you are dependent on someone else, you lose your freedom. You are beholden to their whims because you rely on their support. When you take care of yourself you make your own decisions and decide your own future.

Today ask yourself if you are following God's blueprint for your life. If you are not, how can you get there? Ask God for guidance and support as you get back on track to a happy and peaceful life. Keep calm and carry on...

S.O.S.

Have I not commanded you? Be strong and courageous.
Do not be afraid; do not be discouraged, for the Lord your
God will be with you wherever you go.
Joshua 1:9 NIV

The only survivor of a shipwreck was washed up on a small, uninhabited island. He prayed feverishly for God to rescue him. Every day he scanned the horizon for help, but none seemed forthcoming.

He eventually managed to build a little hut out of driftwood to protect himself from the elements and to store his few possessions. One day, after scavenging for food, he returned home to find his little hut in flames, with smoke rolling up to the sky. He was stunned with disbelief, grief and anger. He cried out, "God! How Could you do this to me?!" Exhausted and distraught, he fell asleep on the cold sand of the beach.

Early the next day he was awakened by the sound of a ship approaching the island. It had come to rescue him! The weary man asked his rescuers, "How did you know I was here?"

They replied, "We saw your smoke signal!"

Remember this story the next time your little hut seems to be burning to the ground. It just may be the hand of God orchestrating your rescue!

Actions Speak Louder...

Dear Children, let us not love with words
or speech but with actions and in truth.
1 John 3:18 NIV

In 1934, St. Louis Cardinals pitcher, Jay Hanna Dean, also known as Dizzy, made a boastful prediction. He said that he and his brother, fellow Cardinals pitcher, Paul "Daffy" Dean, would win forty-five games between the two of them before the season was over. When reporters challenged this bold statement, Dizzy replied, "It ain't bragging if you can back it up!" Not only did Dizzy win thirty games and Daffy win nineteen, but they led the team to a World Championship that year. He *wasn't* bragging. He said he was going to do something and he did it.

What have you said aloud that you have not backed up with action? Do you tell people that you love others more than yourself? Do you tell them that you love God over everything else? Do you support these statements with deeds or are people left wondering if you are all talk and no action?

Today, ask God to give you a way to show your love for Him and for other people today. Ask Him to put someone in your path that needs you, someone that you could help through actions over words. It ain't bragging if you do it!

Son, what kind of pitch would you like to miss?'
-Dizzy Dean

The Lord is My Sherpa

Praise be to the Lord, to God our Savior,
who daily bears our burdens.
Psalm 68:19 NIV

Every year Westerners travel to the mountains of Nepal in central Asia. They go there to climb to the top of Mount Everest, an amazing feat to be sure. But before they even begin their trek, a Sherpa is preparing their way up the mountain.

Sherpas, local people who are highly skilled and experienced climbers, are paid to set up base camps, fix the climbing ropes and carry the necessary equipment up the mountain. They guide the tourists up and take care of them along the way. When the group finally reaches the summit, the exhilarated climbers celebrate this great accomplishment! They made it – with a lot of help from the Sherpas!

God bears our burdens for us so that we, too, can accomplish our goals. He prepares our way, provides us with sustenance, shelter and encouragement. He guides us to the summit where we can all celebrate our great victory with Him!

Today thank the Lord for his guidance and support. You can achieve amazing feats of your own with Him as your guide!

Behind every successful climber
is a Sherpa rolling his eyes.
-anonymous

Bad Day at Black Rock

*But the Lord is faithful, and He will strengthen
you and protect you from the evil one.
2 Thessalonians 3:3 NIV*

My husband went to the garage to grab something from the car. As he stepped through the door he flipped on the light just in time to see his boot come down on top of a big, black scorpion. Needless to say, the scorpion did not survive, but the little pill bug that it was chasing at the time did and he scurried off out of sight. Things did not end up the way either one of those little creatures thought they would!

Sometimes things can look completely hopeless and then suddenly, from out of nowhere, help arrives! The Lord sees when you are in trouble. He is faithful in His protection and strengthening of you.

Today, thank God for His awesome faithfulness! Go forth knowing that you have His strength and protection on your side. He is the giant boot coming down through the darkness to crush the enemy!

Eternally Yours...

*Heaven and earth will pass away,
But my words will never pass away.
Matthew 24:35 NIV*

It is absolutely true that nothing here on earth lasts forever. And that's a good thing! Knowing our suffering will pass helps us get through it. Knowing that this world will pass away keeps us focused on God and His promise of an eternal life with Him.

If you are facing struggles in your life right now, try to step back and look at them from an eternal viewpoint. All of these things that you worry about, all of the people that cause you grief, all of your aches and pains and sicknesses are the things of this temporary world. God is eternal. His word is eternal. His promises are eternal. And because you are the very special and loved child of God, you are eternal, too!

You will outlive this world and all of its problems and imperfections! Today, strive to meet your challenges head-on, without fear, knowing that this is a battle that you have already won!

He Cares For You

Cast all your anxiety on him because he cares for you.
1 Peter 5:7 NIV

Sometimes when I pray I feel a little guilty. Here I am praying about the things that are important to *me* and to *my* family and then it hits me - in the big scheme of things my prayer requests can seem pretty small and unimportant. Surely the Lord has better things to do than listen to my selfish prayers.

I know that there are others who are worse off than I am. I know the world is in turmoil and is in desperate need of prayer. I know that I should put others first. But is it okay to pray for myself and for the things that are important to me personally?

The Bible does not say, "Cast your anxiety on Him...but only if it is something big." No, it says, "Cast *all* your anxiety on Him because He cares for you." There are no restrictions. He wants to hear *your* prayers. He wants to have a personal relationship with *you*!

When God says to give it all to Him, the Bible tells us He means it! Today give all of your cares and worries to God, thanking Him for His everlasting love and kindness!

Is the Futon Ready?

Jesus replied, "*Anyone who loves me will obey my teaching. My Father will love them, and we will come to them and make our home with them.*"
John 14:23 NIV

I had an aunt who used to say, "Guests, like fish, begin to smell after three days." This really worried me because whenever I went back home for Christmas, I usually stayed for a couple of weeks. I must have been really 'smelly' by the time I left! I later learned that this quote originally came from Ben Franklin, so maybe the three-day time limit just came with the quote and wasn't an actual hint to pack up and leave at a certain time. Maybe...

Our Heavenly Father wants to come and make His home with you. He doesn't want to just visit every now and then. He wants to be a part of your life and your decisions. He wants to guide your footsteps and prop you up when you need it. He wants to have a personal one-on-one relationship with you every day, from now on!

Today, let God know how much you love Jesus and ask His help as you strive to obey His teaching. Invite Him to come into your home, not just as a guest, but as a permanent part of your life. You won't regret it!

It Keeps Going and Going

For the Lord is good and His love endures forever; His
faithfulness continues through all generations.
Psalm 100:5 NIV

I have a horrible alarm clock. Every morning, it
blares out a sound that is a cross between a fog horn
and an air-raid siren. Every morning I have a dream
that ends with my cruise ship crashing into an iceberg
or with me running for cover from the Blitz! Then I
realize that it's just time for me to wake up. After lying
there for a bit to catch my breath and let my heart rate
return to normal, I rise and start my day. My first
thought of the morning is that I need to get a new alarm
clock and my second is that I am still really, really tired.

With all the hats that we wear, it is hard to get
enough rest. We work, go to school, study, clean house,
do laundry, attend church and bible study, minister to
our friends and neighbors and much more. We can find
ourselves exhausted with no relief in sight. Where can
we find the extra energy we need to get through the
day?

The Lord is the quintessential, ever-ready battery!
When all those around us tire, give up and quit, the
Lord's faithfulness lasts forever. Through Him, we can
obtain all of the strength and endurance that we will
ever need! Today ask God to keep you energized with the
Holy Spirit so that you, too, can keep going and going!

True Love

Love is patient, love is kind. It does not envy,
it does not boast, it is not proud. It does not dishonor
others, it is not self-seeking, it is not easily angered,
it keeps no record of wrongs.
1 Corinthians 13:4-5 NIV

What comes to mind when you hear the phrase, "true love"? Is it your relationship with your significant other? Or maybe it's the relationship of your grandparents who were married forever? Or are you reminded of fictional characters like Romeo and Juliet, Tristan and Isolde, or The Doctor and River Song?

Have you ever wondered if you truly loved someone else or were truly loved in return? Or wondered what would this love look like and how you could trust it?

The Bible gives us a litmus test for true love. We don't have to wonder about it. Does your love for others contain all of the elements listed in the above verse? Do you feel and express kindness and patience? Do you put the other person first? Do you uplift them? Do you control your envy, pride and anger? Are you truly forgiving, letting bygones be bygones? If not, how can you improve on these things and obtain the true love that you seek?

Now, apply this test to your relationship with God. Do you have a true love for Him? Today ask the Lord to guide you as you strive to have this love for Him and for others.

Dig In

Therefore, my dear brothers and sisters,
stand firm. Let nothing move you. Always give
yourselves fully to the work of the Lord, because you
know that your labor in the Lord is not in vain.
1 Corinthians 15:58

Life is a never ending game of tug-o-war! You can be on a team of 'tuggers' or tug on your own, but either way you are going to be tugging! The opposing team will pull you as hard as they can and you will have to decide if you will be dragged into the trench or if you will dig in and pull back with all of your might.

The enemy uses earthly temptations and sins to pull us away from God's side and over to his. He wants to distract us from doing the Lord's work and take us down into the abyss to wallow in the mire with him. He is vigilant in his assault, so we must be vigilant in our resistance.

The Bible tells us to stand firm. It tells us that we are doing the right thing when we focus on the Lord and his good works. It tells us our labor is not in vain. We must fight the good fight. We must resist and pull back from the things that want to move us!

Today ask the Lord to be the anchor in your personal game of tug-o-war. With Him on your team you will be able to stay true in your work and stand firm against the enemy!

God Don't Make No Junk

For you created my inmost being;
you knit me together in my mother's womb.
I praise you because I am fearfully and wonderfully
made; your works are wonderful, I know that full well.
Psalm 139:13-14 NIV

Why were you created? Was is so you could grow up, get married, have a family, retire and then die? Was it so you could work all day and come home tired every night? Was it so you could constantly worry about your future and the future of your loved ones?

Absolutely not! You were lovingly and wonderfully made by the creator of the Universe! You were given the ability to worship, to sing, to laugh, to feel joy, and to love. You were given unique gifts, a sense of humor, special traits and abilities. No one else has the exact same physical appearance, fingerprints, or DNA. You have grown and evolved based on a life that only you have lived. There truly is only one you!

If you believe that God created the whole world around you, if you recognize it for its absolute wonder and beauty and if you acknowledge that God is all-powerful and all-knowing, then how can you not see *yourself* as an absolute miracle? The same hands that created every awesome thing around you also created you!! We know full well that His works are wonderful!

Today ask God to help you find your real purpose here on this Earth. Ask Him to use your unique gifts and talents for Him. In this way, you will find true joy!

Genuine Genuflection

*It is written: "'As surely as I live,' says the Lord,
'every knee will bow before me;
every tongue will acknowledge God.'"
Romans 14:11 NIV*

When I was a child I was taught that I could pray anywhere. I didn't have to be in church or Sunday school. I could be in the park and pray while I played. I could pray in the backseat of the car or while hanging upside down from a tree or lying in my bed. I had a direct line to God and I just needed to use it!

One night I went to a friend's house for a sleepover. When it was time to go to bed I put on my pajamas, brushed my teeth and climbed in under the covers. I started to say my nightly prayer in my head when I heard my friend praying out loud.

I looked over and saw that she was kneeling on the floor next to the bed with her head bowed and hands clasped. She finished saying her prayer and jumped into bed.

"You know," I said smartly, "you don't have to do all that to pray to God. You can get comfortable in bed and then pray."

"I know," she replied. "But after everything He has done for me, the very least I can do is kneel when I pray."

The beauty and simplicity of that statement has stayed with me ever since. Yes, I can and do pray anywhere, but there is something wonderful about kneeling before God. Today, when you go to the Lord in prayer, try kneeling and see how focused on Him you become.

Safe Haven

*I will say of the Lord, "He is my refuge
and my fortress, my God, in whom I trust."*
Psalm 91:2 NIV

In the 80's, there was a television commercial for Calgon bath oil beads. In the ad, a frazzled mother is experiencing a very hectic day and in desperation she calls out, "Calgon! Take me away!" In the next scene, we see her relaxing in a warm bathtub full of luxurious bubbles without a care in the world. She smiles directly into the camera and says, "It's paradise!"

That slogan became a mantra for me. Whenever my work or home became hectic or overwhelming I would place the back of my hand against my forehead and say, "Calgon! Take me away!" And even though I didn't end up in a real bubble bath, I felt better because I imagined myself in one. (Of course, the kids wondered who Calgon was and if I'd be back in time to make dinner.)

The next time you get stressed and need to take a little mental vacation, remember that we have more than just a "happy place" to go to. We can go to a true refuge, a fortress from the world that is our Lord. A place where we are safe and loved and where can find true peace whenever we need it!

Hang in There, Baby!

You need to persevere so that when you have done the
will of God, you will receive what He has promised.
Hebrews 10:35 NIV

Have you ever seen the poster of a cute, little kitten dangling precariously by its claws from a tree branch over the words "Hang In There Baby"? I bet you have felt like that kitten at some point in your life. I know I have!

Because I love happy endings I always wanted another poster to hang next to that one. In this poster, the same kitten is sitting happily on top of the branch contentedly licking her front paw. Her expression shows that, yes, she was scared for a moment, but then she realized that she had all the tools necessary to triple-lindy herself back to safety. She used the gifts God had given her and persevered!!

We don't have cat-like reflexes and retractable claws, but we do have other tools to help us hang in there when necessary. Today ask God for perseverance while you strive to do His will, knowing that when you are finished His wonderful promises await you!

True Value

I once thought these things were valuable, but now I consider them worthless because of what Christ has done. Yes, everything else is worthless when compared with the infinite value of knowing Christ Jesus my Lord. For his sake I have discarded everything else, counting it all as garbage, so that I could gain Christ.
Philippians 3:7-8 NLT

One day my son called me from college in another state to tell me he had been in a car accident. I can assure you that my first question was not, "Is the *car* okay?" or even, "Who's fault was it?" When things like this happen, we realize what is truly important in our lives. Thankfully, in this case, no one was hurt, but it made me consider the value that we put on *things*.

Likewise, when we realize what Christ did for us, how He came to live among us to teach us and guide us, how He suffered the humiliation and agony of the crucifixion, and how He defeated death so that we may receive from Him an eternal life, well, everything else just seems so insignificant!

I doubt that there are many, if any, people who lie on their death beds and wish that they had more stuff. I imagine that when that day comes, they wish for more time. Not more time for a manicure or a shopping trip or a new car, but more time with loved ones. The things that they have accumulated through the years will be as valuable as garbage. After all, you really can't take it with you – and you won't want to!

Today, thank God for all of the things that you have, then assign the appropriate amount of importance to those things. Put them low on the priorities list. Thank God for the all of the blessings of true value in your life: your relationship with Him, your family and your friends. You are blessed indeed!

He Walked a Mile In Your Sandals

*For we do not have a high priest who is unable to
empathize with our weaknesses,
but we have one who has been tempted in every way,
just as we are-yet he did not sin.
Hebrews 4:15 NIV*

God gave us the perfect example of how to live our lives when He sent His son to dwell with us on earth. That is why, as Christians, one of our goals is to be Christ-like in all that we do. Although we know that we will never attain this goal completely, we reach for it anyway because the reaching brings us closer to God.

Jesus lived among us as a man for 33 years. He faced hunger, thirst, fatigue, pain, and temptation just like we do. He did not succumb to temptation, but He knows how it feels like to be tempted. He empathizes with our weaknesses. He understands us and what it means to be us.

We will never be able to resist all the temptations that the enemy puts in our paths the way that Jesus did, but that doesn't mean that we shouldn't try. Each time that we resist and prevail we have achieved another victory over sin!

Today, thank the Lord that He sent His son to live among us, to show us how to live here on earth and how to live eternally with Him in Heaven. Thank Him for His understanding and empathy towards us and ask Him to guide you as you face down today's temptations.

The Way,

For Christ also suffered once for sins, the righteous for the unrighteous, to bring you to God. He was put to death in the body but made alive in the Spirit.
1 Peter 3:18 NIV

I finally traded in my flip phone for one of those hand-held marvels that my kids carry around. One of my favorite features on this new phone is the map app. I tell it where I want to go and it gives me complete and precise directions and if I miss a turn it very politely tells me so. It also speaks in a British accent and calls me, "Foxy", thanks to my youngest daughter who set up that feature and won't tell me how to change it. So whenever I get lost James Bond says, "Make a u-turn now, Foxy!"

The Bible is a map app for Christians. How do we get to where we want to be? Well, Foxy, Jesus Christ is the way! He is the way to God, our Father. He is the way to an eternal life. He is the way to victory over sin. He is the way to inner peace. He is the way to abundant joy. He is the way to knowledge. He is the way to wisdom of the ages. He is the way to strength that moves mountains. He is the way to speech that changes hearts. He is the way to ultimate triumph over the enemy. We can never be lost when we follow Him!

Today, thank God for giving us complete and precise directions to follow in order to reach Him. Thank Him for sending His son to live among us and to die for us so that we can have a way to our ultimate destination, eternal life with heavenly Father!

The Truth,

For I am not ashamed of the gospel, because it is the power of God that brings salvation to everyone who believes; first to the Jews, then to the Gentile.
Romans 1:16 NIV

Are you ashamed of being a Christian? Are you embarrassed to tell others what you believe when you are confronted at work or school? Do you wait to be asked directly before you admit your faith or do you offer it up freely?

In recent years, there has been a harsh and obvious change in our society that trends towards secular beliefs and away from Christianity. It used to be embarrassing to get caught doing or saying something that was contrary to Biblical teachings. It was considered wrong to bad-mouth your parents, friends, school or church. It was wrong to take the Lord's name in vain. If you stole or lied or cheated there were negative social consequences. Now if you do these things, you are considered edgy or deep. And if you are really bad? You get your own reality show!

Do not let the world get you discouraged! You know the truth and the truth never changes! You are saved by the blood of the lamb now and forever! Social norms and societal pressures will continuously change. But the truth of your salvation never will!

Today thank the Lord for the never-ending, never-changing, all-powerful truth of the gospel. Ask Him to help you share your faith with others and to bless your efforts as you proudly proclaim His truth to those around you.

...And The Life

Surely God is my salvation; I will trust and not be afraid.
The Lord, the Lord Himself, is my strength and my
defense; He has become my salvation.
Isaiah 12:2 NIV

I am not a very good flyer. I become nervous from the moment the trip has been planned and the airplane tickets have been purchased until the moment we have landed safely at the airport. And then, I am sad to say, my wonderful vacation is punctuated by moments of panic when thoughts of the flight back home creep into my mind.

I do not have a good reason for this fear. I fully understand that I have a better chance of being struck by lightening or of getting into a car accident on the way to the airport than I do of being in a plane crash. And I certainly would never let my children get on board if I truly believed something bad would happen. So, even though I am afraid, we get on the plane anyway. I trust that we will get to our destination unscathed. But, I am ashamed to say, I do not trust without fear.

Why do we let fear control so much of our lives? When we are afraid, we don't always think clearly. We don't enjoy things, we don't focus on the goodness around us. We are distracted from doing God's work.

The next time you are afraid, remember that you have the ultimate safety net! The Lord Himself is your strength and your defense! Today, ask God to decrease your fears and increase your trust in Him. He is your Salvation! What more could you need?

Wear a Chest Protector

Above all else, guard your heart,
for everything you do flows from it.
Proverbs 4:23 NIV

One summer we were getting my son geared up for Little League Baseball. In our cart we had a batting helmet and glove, a catcher's mitt, catcher's equipment, uniform pants, warm-up pants, belt, socks, cleats, a bat and practice balls. As we were shopping, a sales associate walked over with a small box in her hand and said, "Don't forget your Heart Guard!" She gave us the box and walked away. In all our years of baseball parenting, we had never heard of this piece of equipment. It turns out that there is a one in five million chance that your child could get hit in the chest with a baseball and if that happens, you want him to be wearing one of these.

I am sure that in the future the word *sports* will mean wrapping your child from head to toe in bubble wrap and gently placing him into a netted enclosure full of marshmallows. Once inside, all participants will hurl compliments at each other until everyone is declared the winner and given the exact same trophy. Until then, they have helmets, pads, and heart guards.

The Bible says to guard your heart because everything you do flows from it. If you keep God's commands within your heart, then your words and works will be good. Today, ask God to guard your heart against sin and evil. Keep yourself safely bubble-wrapped in the commands and promises of the Lord!

What Is A Million Dollars Worth?

And my God will supply every need of yours according to
His riches in glory in Christ Jesus.
Phillipians 4:19 ESV

I know your afflictions and your poverty—
yet you are rich!
Revelation 2:9a NIV

What *is* a million dollars worth? At first, that question doesn't seem to make any sense. A million dollars is worth, well, a million dollars. But that's not really my question to you. Have you ever thought about what you would do with that kind of money at your disposal? Would you buy a new car, designer clothes, or travel the world? Money seems so important when you think of all the *stuff* you could buy.

What if you were offered a million dollars right now in exchange for your salvation? One of your family members? One of your friends? Your health? Years from your life? Money has no value when compared to the true treasures in life.

When you think of money this way, you realize that you are already, truly, rich indeed! Today thank God for the true riches that He has so generously blessed you with.

...But Will You?

In all toil there is profit,
but mere talk tends only to poverty.
Proverbs 14:23 ESV

When my youngest daughter was thirteen, she wanted to earn some money. Babysitting jobs were scarce, so she started a little jewelry making business. She made pendants, keychains and magnets to sell at local craft fairs. She did pretty well and I enjoyed spending time with her at her table.

One thing we heard over and over was, "I could make that myself". Browsing customers would inspect the merchandise and then say to one another how easy it would be to make this or that themselves. And then they would move on without purchasing anything. I noticed that one of our fellow crafters, out of frustration, made a sign for her table that simply said, "I know you *can*, but *will* you?" Suddenly her sales dramatically increased!

Are there things that you have talked about doing, but never have? Is there a 'someday' project that you have been meaning to do? A book you've been wanting to write? A language you've wanted to learn? An instrument you would like to play? Why wait any longer? Today is your someday – make it happen!

Global Extreme Warming Ice Age

*It is He who made the earth by His power,
who established the world by His wisdom,
and by His understanding stretched out the heavens.
When He utters His voice, there is a tumult of waters in
the heavens, and He makes the mist rise from the ends of
the earth. He makes lightning for the rain, and He brings
forth the wind from His storehouses.*
Jeremiah 10: 12-13 ESV

Isn't it a beautiful day? I don't know if it is raining, snowing, blowing, sleeting or shining where you are right now, but I do know that it is glorious! It would be so boring to have the same weather day after day. We would miss out on the delicious smell of rain, the thrill of thunder and lightening, the pure white beauty of the new fallen snow. Each is a masterpiece created by the designer of the universe.

In the 1970's we were told that we were heading into a new ice age. In the late 1990's we were told the earth was warming too quickly. Today we have "global extreme weather", which includes anything and everything weather related.

Some scientists say these changes are cyclical and occur naturally and some say they are caused by mankind. Some say there aren't any real changes at all, just trumped up weather reports to fit a political agenda.

Whatever you choose to believe about these conflicting reports, remember that God is in charge of all things big and small. Today give praise to God for the glorious weather that has formed and shaped our earth since the beginning of time, that has created the environment that we live in and that reminds us of God's magnificent power!

You Might Want to Walk That Back a Little

But, "Let the one who boasts boast in the Lord." For it is not the one who commends himself who is approved, but the one whom the Lord commends.
2 Corinthians 10:17-18

In the future, science has advanced to the point where man believes he knows everything there is about DNA, RNA, cell structure and the origin of life. He even believes he has mastered the art of creation itself. One day he calls out to the Lord, "Hey, God, we don't need you anymore! We have figured out how to create life on our own!"

"Show me," the Lord replies.

The man reaches down and picks up a handful of dirt and... is immediately interrupted.

"Not so fast," says the Lord. "Get your own dirt."

The Bible tells us to boast in the Lord and not in ourselves. We should remember that everything we accomplish results from the gifts that He has given us. Today, thank the Lord for the initiative, motivation, judgment, talents, intellect, wisdom, physical ability and the raw material that He has bestowed upon you. He has made it possible for you to achieve great things. When you do something to be proud of – feel proud, but if you feel like boasting about it, make sure you give credit where credit is due. Boast in the Lord and let your commendations come from Him.

Clean Up in Aisle Three

May the God of hope fill you with all joy
and peace as you trust in Him,
so that you may overflow with hope
by the power of the Holy Spirit.
Romans 15:13 NIV

What would it feel like to overflow with hope? To radiate joy? To bask in peace? To tingle with the electricity of unknown possibility, yet have faith that everything will turn out for the glory of the Lord? You can have all of this just by placing your trust in the Lord!

What do you hope for? Is it a better future? A peaceful world? The end to suffering? Christ's return? Your hopes are not in vain! All of these things will come to pass in God's time.

Today ask the God of hope, our heavenly Father, to fill you with peace and joy. Tell Him your hopes for yourself, your family and the world. Ask Him for an overflowing hope for the future and thank Him for being in control of all that has happened, is happening and will happen!

Hope is the pillar that holds up the world.
Hope is the dream of a waking man.
-Pliny the Elder

Return the Favor

May my meditation be pleasing to him,
for I rejoice in the LORD.
Psalm 104:34 ESV

When we take time to do our daily devotion and prayer we are reaching out to Heaven, seeking fellowship with the Lord. We want His guidance on something, His help with something or we want Him to grant us a miracle. Sometimes we reach out to Him with thanksgiving and praise, with no agenda at all. Whatever the reason for your devotion and prayer, you are reaching out to Him as He has asked you to.

David prayed that his daily devotion (or meditation) would bring joy to the Lord. The Lord was the reason for David's joy and he wanted to return the favor. He didn't want this treasured time to only benefit him, he wanted God to be pleased as well.

When working on your personal relationship with the Lord, remember that relationships are two-way streets. Ask God for the things you want and need. Praise Him for all of His many blessings. But in all things, try to be pleasing to the Lord. Reciprocate His goodness and love.

Today, thank God for His presence in your life and for the relationship that you share. Ask Him to guide your actions today so that they are pleasing to Him. Successful relationships require the effort of both parties. God is holding up his end, are you?

The Best (Verse) For Last

For God so loved the world, that he gave his only begotten Son, that whosoever believeth in him should not perish, but have everlasting life.
John 3:16 KJV

Most Christians have a favorite Bible verse, the one they live by, the one that they go to in times of trouble or times of praise. Maybe you have several verses that you keep in your heart, ready to pull out when needed.

You can find guidance in the Bible for every situation that you will face in your life. Many Bibles have an index in the back where you can look up any subject and find a verse that addresses it: love, joy, pain, money, work, grief, politics, laughter, just about anything under the sun is in there. But is there one verse that is more important than any other?

For me, John 3:16 sums everything up in one simple statement. It lets us know how vast and deep God's love is for us. It tells us of God's sacrifice, the life of His only son for our salvation. It gives us hope for our future with the promise of an everlasting life. This verse makes us realize how important we are and how unimportant the things of this world are. We are made worthy of His love by His sacrifice and we have been gifted, through no act of our own, an everlasting life with our Lord. What more can you add to that?!

Today thank the Lord for His word. Thank Him that we can find answers to our questions by studying the Bible. Thank Him for the sacrifice that He made on our behalf and for the promise of eternal life that he has given us. Strive to live your life as one who is worthy of such love, seeking guidance, forgiveness, patience and knowledge. Praise Him in all things and keep moving Heavenward!

Notes:

Recipes

Cherubic Cherry Berry Smoothie

Cherubic Cherry-Berry Smoothie

1 cups cherry juice
1- 8 oz cartons vanilla yogurt (Greek or reg.)
1 cup frozen, unsweetened raspberries
½ cup seedless red grapes
½ cup fresh or frozen blueberries
1-2 tbsp honey or equivalent amt. sweetener

Directions:

Combine all ingredients in blender. Blend until smooth and creamy. Pour into two large glasses and serve immediately.

Veritable Veritas Veggie Scramble

Veritable Veritas Veggie Scramble

Ingredients:

1 medium zucchini, peeled and diced
1-2 cups fresh baby spinach leaves
½ small tomato, diced
½ small onion, chopped
½ large red bell pepper, chopped
½ cup sliced mushrooms
1 tbsp butter
6 eggs
¼ cup milk
salt and pepper to taste
½ cup shredded cheese, if desired

Directions:

In large frying pan, melt butter. Add zucchini and onion. Saute until zucchini starts to soften and onion starts to become transparent. Add bell pepper and mushrooms and cook all until desired consistency.

In a large mixing bowl, whisk together eggs, milk, salt and pepper. Pour over vegetables and scramble until eggs are firm. Remove from heat and sprinkle with cheese, if desired. Serves 2-4.

Youthful Yogurt Parfait

Be Ye Gracious Homemade Granola

Youthful Yogurt Parfait

6 oz vanilla or strawberry lo-fat yogurt
¾ cup homemade granola (p 88)
½ cup fresh or frozen blueberries
½ cup fresh or frozen strawberries sliced
¼ cup fresh or frozen whole blackberries

Directions:

Layer in a tall glass or mug from the bottom up:

¼ cup granola
3 oz yogurt
¼ cup granola
¼ cup blueberries
¼ cup strawberries
3 oz yogurt
¼ cup granola
¼ cup blueberries
¼ cup strawberries
¼ cup blackberries

Chill. Enjoy!

Be Ye Gracious
Homemade Granola

Ingredients:

5 cups old-fashioned oats
1 cup brown sugar
1 cup flaked coconut
1 cup wheat germ
1 tbsp ground cinnamon
1 tsp ground nutmeg
½ cup water
½ cup canola oil
1 tbsp vanilla extract
½ cup dried fruit (raisins, cranberries, mangoes, etc.)
½ cup nuts (almonds, pecans, cashews, etc.

Directions:

Preheat oven to 325F°.

In large mixing bowl, stir together oats, sugar, coconut, wheat germ, cinnamon and nutmeg until well blended.

In small bowl, stir together water, oil and vanilla extract. Pour over oat mixture and stir well. Pour onto a baking sheet coated with cooking spray.

Bake for approximately 1 hour, stirring well every 15 minutes. When golden brown, remove from oven and cool on pan. Transfer to a large container, stir in nuts and fruit. Serve with milk, frozen yogurt or on top of Amen Apple Crisp or in Youthful Yogurt Parfait.

Bring On the Glory Breakfast Sandwich

Brand New Day Breakfast Burritos

Bring On the Glory
Breakfast Sandwich

Ingredients:

4 leftover dinner rolls
4 breakfast sausage patties
4 slices of cheese, any kind
4 eggs
hot sauce

Directions:

Preheat oven to *Broil*.

Slice open rolls, place all halves face up on cookie sheet. Lay 1/2 slice of cheese on top of each. Set aside.

In frying pan, cook patty sausage until done in the middle and slightly crispy on the outside. Remove to plate covered with a paper towel to drain excess grease.

In a separate pan, fry eggs to desired doneness.

Put rolls in oven under broiler. Watch constantly and remove when cheese is melted and bubbly.

Place one sausage patty onto the bottom half of each roll then top sausage with an egg. Sprinkle each with hot sauce. Place top half of rolls over the eggs and serve immediately.

Brand New Day
Breakfast Burritos

Ingredients:

½ lb. breakfast sausage
1 16 oz pkg frozen hash browns, southern style
2 tbsp butter
12 eggs
1 cup sliced green onions
3 cups shredded cheese (cheddar or Monterey Jack)
12 flour tortillas, burrito size, warm

Directions:

Preheat oven to 350F°.

In a medium skillet, brown sausage according to package instructions. Drain grease and set aside.

In large skillet, brown hash browns according to package instructions. Set hash aside in a bowl, saving skillet for next steps.

In large mixing bowl, beat eggs until blended. Stir in green onions. Melt butter in the large skillet then add eggs, cook stirring constantly until eggs are set.

Add sausage and hash browns to scrambled eggs, mix well. Put ¾ cup filling and ¼ cup of cheese on top of each warm tortilla. Roll them into burritos and place them on a greased cookie sheet. Bake for 15 minutes.

Wrap leftover burritos in plastic wrap and foil, freeze. When ready to eat, discard foil and plastic. Wrap in a paper towel and microwave for 1–2 minutes.

Prayer and Peanut Butter Pancakes

Bountiful Earth Blueberry Muffins

Prayer and Peanut Butter Pancakes

Ingredients:

1 cup flour
2 1/2 teaspoons baking powder
1/2 teaspoon salt
1/2 cup creamy peanut butter
2 tablespoons sugar
2 tablespoons vegetable oil
1 large egg
1 cup plus 2 tablespoons milk
Banana slices (optional)
Honey roasted peanuts, coarsely chopped (optional)
Maple syrup

Directions:

In a large bowl, mix together flour, baking powder, and salt, and set aside.

In a small bowl, whisk together the peanut butter, sugar, and oil until smooth. Beat in the egg, then the milk. Pour the wet mixture into the dry mixture, stirring just until blended.

Pour batter by ¼ cupfuls onto lightly greased hot griddle. Cook until small bubbles appear on surface, then flip and cook a few minutes more.

Serve topped with sliced bananas, chopped peanuts and maple syrup. Makes 10–12 pancakes.

Bountiful Earth
Blueberry Muffins

Ingredients:

3 cups flour
¼ cup sugar + 1 tbsp for topping
1 ½ tbsp. baking powder
¾ tsp. salt
2 eggs, beaten
1 ½ cups buttermilk
6 tbsp. butter or margarine, softened
1 ½ tsp. vanilla
1 ½ cup blueberries (lightly coated in flour)

Directions:

Preheat oven to 350F° and grease muffin tin. In mixing bowl, stir together flour, sugar, baking powder and salt. Make a well in center of dry ingredients.

In another bowl, stir together eggs, buttermilk, butter and vanilla. Pour into dry ingredient well and then stir, do not over mix. Batter will be lumpy. Fold blueberries into batter.

Fill muffin tins ¾ full. If desired, sprinkle with sugar. Bake for 20 minutes or until golden brown. Makes 12 muffins.

Sweet Embrace Empanadas

Steadfast Sticky Buns

Sweet Embrace Empanadas

Ingredients:

3 cups flour
2 tsp. baking powder
½ tsp. salt
3 tbsp. sugar
½ cup shortening
½ cup milk
1 cup of your favorite jam or jelly
Extra sugar to sprinkle on top

Directions:

Preheat oven to 350F°. In large bowl, mix together flour, baking powder, salt and sugar. Using a fork, cut in shortening. Add milk and beat until dough starts to form. Using hands, shape dough into ball.

On a lightly floured surface, roll dough out to 1/8" thickness and cut into 4" circles. In the center of each place 2 tablespoons of jam, then fold in half. Using a fork dipped in water, seal edges.

Sprinkle with sugar and bake for 20 minutes or until golden brown.

*Instead of jam, stuff these with leftover taco meat or ground breakfast sausage and cheese for a delicious snack or lunch.

Steadfast Sticky Buns

Ingredients:

½ cup butter, melted
½ cup packed brown sugar
2 cans refrigerator biscuits or French loaf dough
¼ cup sugar
2 tsp. ground cinnamon

Directions:

Preheat oven to 350F°. Grease 12-cup muffin tin.

Stir brown sugar into the melted butter until it is smooth and spoon 1 tablespoon of this carmel into each muffin cup. Set aside.

Open biscuits, separate and cut each one into 5 or 6 picces. If using the French loaf dough, cut or tear dough into 1" pieces.

In a gallon bag, mix together sugar and cinnamon.
Add dough to bag and shake well to coat each piece thoroughly. Place 7–10 pieces of dough into each muffin cup.

Bake for 12 – 15 minutes or until golden brown. Let rest for 1 minute then turn upside down onto large serving plate. Serve warm.

Champion Chicken Salad

Stand Firm Stuffed
Micro-Baked Potato

Champion Chicken Salad

Ingredients:

1 8oz can pineapple chunks
2 Tbsp juice from pineapple
2/3 cup mayonnaise
1 Tbsp Dijon mustard
1/8 tsp salt
4 cups cooked chicken, diced*
1 cup grapes
¾ cup celery, thinly sliced
1 green onion, sliced
1/3 cup walnuts (or any nut)

Directions:

In a small bowl, mix pineapple juice, mayo, mustard and salt. Set aside.

In a large bowl, combine remaining ingredients and stir well. Add mayonnaise mixture, mix well and chill for at least one hour. Salt and pepper to taste.

Serve on bread, lettuce or alone. Makes 4 servings.

*You can also use frozen grilled-and-diced chicken found in the freezer section of the grocery store or canned chicken.

Stand Firm Stuffed Micro-Baked Potato

Ingredients:

1 large Russet, Idaho, yellow or baking potato
½ cup shredded cheese
½ cup diced onion or chives
2 Tbsp bacon bits
1 dollop of sour cream

Directions:

Wash potato thoroughly with cold, running water. Scrub with vegetable brush, if necessary, to remove all loose dirt. Pat dry. Brush peel lightly with olive oil and sprinkle with salt.

Place on microwave-safe plate. Pierce several times all over with a fork. Microwave on high for 5 minutes. Turn over and cook for another 3 to 5 minutes. It is done when a fork can slide in easily, but potato still feels a little firm.

Flatten top slightly with a spatula, slice along top and press ends in towards the middle to force open. Stuff with remaining ingredients.

Don't forget to eat the peel – it is full of nutrients!

Be Ye Fishers of Men Fish Tacos

Be Ye Fishers of Men Fish Tacos

Ingredients:

4-6 frozen fish filets (breaded cod or grilled tilapia)
12 small corn tortillas
1 small bag shredded cabbage (or shred yourself)
4 green onions or ½ small white onion, diced
1 small bunch cilantro
1 lime, cut into wedges

Sauce:

½ cup mayonnaise or sour cream
¼ cup salsa
lime juice to taste

Directions:

In small bowl, combine all sauce ingredients and mix well. Set aside in refrigerator.

Bake fish according to directions. Place on plate with paper towels to drain excess grease.

Take 2 tortillas and stack one on top of the other. Place fish filet on tortillas and top with a little sauce, cabbage, onion and cilantro. Take lime wedge and squeeze juice over top. Fold in half and enjoy!

Serve with guacamole and chips, if desired.

Brand New Life Broccoli Cheese Soup

Positive Attitude Potato Cheese Soup

Brand New Life Broccoli Cheese Soup

Ingredients:

10oz broccoli florets (the top part of broccoli, no stems)
3 Tbsp butter
3 Tbsp flour
4 cups milk
4-6 slices of American cheese
salt and pepper to taste
¼ cup shredded cheddar cheese

Directions:

In a large sauce pan, boil broccoli for 5 minutes, drain and set aside in a bowl.

In the same pan, melt butter over medium heat. Stir in flour and mix well. Cook for another 2 minutes then add 1 cup of milk, stirring until smooth. Add remaining milk and cook for 7 – 10 minutes, stirring occasionally.

Reduce heat to low and add salt, pepper and American cheese. Stir until cheese is melted then add broccoli. Mix well. Sprinkle shredded cheese on top for garnish. Makes 4 servings.

Positive Attitude Potato Cheese Soup

Ingredients:

2 medium potatoes (Russet, Idaho, yellow or baking)
6 Tbsp butter
1 medium onion, diced
½ cup flour
2 cups milk
2 ½ cups chicken broth (canned or granules with water)
salt and pepper to taste
8oz shredded cheddar cheese

Directions:

Wash, peel and cut potatoes into bite sized cubes. Set aside.

In a large saucepan, melt butter over medium heat. Add onions and potatoes and sauté for 10 minutes. Stir in flour, mix well. Add one cup of milk and stir until smooth. Gradually add the rest of the milk and the chicken broth. Stirring constantly, bring to a boil, then reduce heat to low. Cover and cook for 20 more minutes, stirring occasionally. Add salt, pepper and cheese, stirring until melted and creamy. If desired, garnish with bacon bits, chives, shredded cheese and sour cream. Makes 4 servings.

Lead the Charge Chicken Caesar Wrap

Lead the Charge Chicken Caesar Wrap

Ingredients:

4 large tortillas or wraps
8 Tbsp bottled Caesar dressing (lite or regular)
4 large leaves Romaine lettuce
2 medium tomatoes, cut into thin wedges
1 cucumber, peeled and cut into long spears
2 cups cooked, diced chicken
2 Tbsp bacon bits
salt and pepper to taste

Directions:

Spread 2 Tbsp dressing evenly in center of each tortilla. Place one lettuce leaf on each. Divide tomato, cucumber, chicken and bacon bits evenly among the tortillas and place on top of lettuce leaves. Salt and pepper to taste.

Fold one edge of each tortilla up 2" to create a cup for your filling. This is the bottom. Then starting at one side, roll tortilla around filling, holding the 'cup' in place. Serve with extra dressing. Makes 4 wraps.

Inner Strength Straw and Hay

Mighty Mandarin and
Grape Tossed Salad

Inner Strength Straw and Hay

Ingredients:

2 Tbsp butter
¼ cup onion, diced
1 ½ cups sliced fresh mushrooms (or canned)
1 cup ham, dice
1 cup heavy cream
salt and pepper to taste
6 oz spinach fettuccine
6 oz regular (egg) fettuccine
parmesan cheese and fresh parsley to garnish

Directions:

In a large skillet, melt butter. Add onion and sauté until tender. Add mushrooms and ham and cook until mushrooms are tender. Slowly stir in cream, mixing until smooth. Add salt and pepper. Reduce heat to low and cook an additional 15 minutes or until thick.

While sauce is cooking, boil fettuccine according to package directions until al dente (done but slightly chewy). Drain. Add to sauce pan and toss until well covered. Garnish with parmesan cheese and fresh parsley if desired.

Mighty Mandarin and Grape Tossed Salad

Ingredients:

10 cups baby spinach
2 11oz cans mandarin oranges drained
2 cups seedless grapes (any kind)
¼ cup red onion diced
1 cup cashews (regular or honey-roasted)
1 Tbsp sesame seeds

Dressing:

¼ cup salad oil (canola or olive)
¼ cup honey
½ tsp brown mustard (or ground mustard seed)
Juice from one lime
Salt and pepper to taste

Directions:

In a large salad bowl, toss together all salad ingredients, except for nuts and seeds. Set aside

In a small bowl or cruet, combine all dressing ingredients. Mix well, pour over salad and toss well. Top with cashews and sesame seeds.

Hope Eternal Honey Chicken

No More Fear 'Not-Fried' Chicken

Hope Eternal Honey Chicken

Ingredients:

8 chicken drumsticks and/or thighs
1/4 cup honey
½ tsp garlic powder
¼ tsp red pepper flakes

Directions:

Preheat oven to 400F°.

In small bowl mix honey, garlic and pepper flakes until well blended. Set aside.

Rinse chicken well and pat dry with paper towels. Place side-by-side in a 9x13 baking dish. Do not overlap pieces. Bake for 30 minutes. Remove from oven and brush honey mixture evenly over each piece. Return to oven and bake for 15 - 20 minutes more or until golden brown. (Make sure chicken is no longer pink.) Serve with a salad and vegetables.

No More Fear 'Not-Fried' Chicken

Ingredients:

½ cup sour cream
1 Tbsp lemon juice
1 tsp Worcestershire sauce
½ tsp garlic salt
4 chicken breasts
1 pkg herb stuffing mix
¼ cup melted butter

Directions:

Preheat oven to 350F°.

In a shallow bowl, mix sour cream, lemon juice, Worcestershire, and garlic salt.

Pour stuffing mix into a gallon storage bag and crush until very fine. Dip chicken into liquid mixture and then put into stuffing bag one at a time to coat thoroughly.

Coat a baking dish with cooking spray. Place chicken in dish side by side. Drizzle with melted butter and bake for 1 hour. Serve with steamed vegetables.

Pray for Peace Pecan Crusted Salmon

Pray for Peace Pecan-Crusted Salmon or Halibut

Ingredients:

4 6oz salmon or halibut fillets
2 cups milk
1 cup finely chopped pecans
½ cup flour
1/3 cup brown sugar, packed
salt and pepper to taste
2 Tbsp cooking oil

Preheat oven to 400F° for salmon, 350F° for halibut.

Place filets in a shallow baking dish. Cover with milk and let stand for 10 minutes in refrigerator.

Meanwhile, in a shallow dish, combine all other ingredients except for oil. When fish is done soaking, drain and discard milk. Coat each filet evenly with the pecan mixture, press into fish to make stick.

In large skillet, heat the oil on medium heat. Put filets in pan and brown both sides.

Rinse milk residue from baking dish, dry and coat with cooking spray or line with foil. Place browned fish back into dish and bake for 8 – 10 minutes until flaky. Serve with rice. Makes 4 servings.

-For halibut, you can substitute crushed macadamia nuts for the pecans.

Evening Grace Easy Roast Beef

Shredded Beef Burritos

BBQ Beef Slider

Evening Grace Easy Roast Beef

Ingredients:

1-2 pound roast (chuck, round, or loin)
1 pkt Lipton onion soup mix
1-2 cups water

Directions:

Coat inside of crock pot with non-stick spray or line with a crock pot liner. Place roast in center of pot. Add water half-way up the side of the roast. Do not cover completely! Sprinkle onion soup mix on top of meat.

Cook on low setting, 8 to 10 hours. Place roast in a large serving dish and shred it with a fork. Remove and discard fat. If meat is too dry, pour some of the juices from the pot over the shredded beef to moisten.

Serve:

Wrap shredded beef in flour tortilla with lettuce, tomato, shredded cheese, onions and salsa to make a burrito.

Serve on hamburger or slider buns with bbq sauce, onions, pickles and coleslaw.

Sprinkle over tortilla chips and melted cheese. Add onions, tomatoes, black olives, jalapenos and sour cream.

Stir into oriental or beef-flavored ramen noodle soup. Add green onions and red pepper flakes.

Revel and Rejoice Ramen

Ingredients:

1 - 2 tbsp butter, olive oil or coconut oil
1 small chicken breast, cut into small cubes
1/4 cup diced carrots
1/4 cup diced onions, white or green
1/4 cup diced zucchini
2 cups water
1 pkg ramen noodles, oriental or chicken flavor

Directions:

In medium saucepan, melt butter (or preheat oil). Add chicken and sauté until no longer pink. Add carrots, onions, zucchini. Saute until vegetable are firm-tender. Add water and bring to boil. Add ramen noodles and sauce packet. Boil for 3 minutes. Makes 2 servings

Amen Apple Crisp

Amen Apple Crisp

Ingredients:

4 cups apples, pared and sliced
¼ cup orange juice
1 cup sugar
¾ cup flour
½ tsp. cinnamon
¼ tsp. nutmeg
½ cup butter
dash of salt

Directions:

Preheat oven to 375F°. Mound apples in buttered 9" pie plate. Sprinkle with orange juice.

Combine sugar, flour, spices and salt. Cut butter into mix with fork until mixture is crumbly. Sprinkle over apples.

Bake for 45 minutes or until apples are tender and topping is crisp. Serve over vanilla yoghurt, oatmeal, pancakes or crepes. Makes 6 servings.

Be Bold Buckeyes

Deliciously Devine Dump Cake

Be Bold Buckeyes

Ingredients:

1 ½ cups creamy peanut butter
½ cup salted butter, softened
1 tsp vanilla
3 cups powdered sugar
1 12oz pkg chocolate chips
2 Tbsp shortening

Directions:

In large bowl, mix peanut butter, butter and vanilla with a hand mixer on low until creamy and well-blended. Add sugar one cup at a time, stirring well. Form into 1" round balls and place on a waxed-paper lined cookie sheet. Refrigerate for at least 15 minutes.

Put chocolate chips and shortening in microwave-safe bowl and microwave on high for 30 seconds. Stir well and microwave for another 30 seconds. Stir until smooth. If not melted enough, cook longer in 10 second intervals, stirring each time and being careful not to burn chocolate.

Stick toothpick into a peanut butter ball and dip into chocolate leaving top of ball uncovered. Place back onto waxed paper. Repeat for all balls and refrigerate until firm.

(You may have to re-melt chocolate during dipping step, as it cools quickly. Re-heat in 10 second intervals only.)

Deliciously Devine Dump Cake

Ingredients:

2 21oz cans cherry pie filling
1 pkg white cake mix
1 2.25oz bag of chopped pecans
2 sticks of butter, melted

Directions:

Preheat oven to 350F°.

Coat 9x11 baking dish with non-stick cooking spray.

Dump both cans of pie filling into pan. Spread evenly. Dump whole box of cake mix on top of filling, spread mix evenly, but do not stir into filling. Sprinkle nuts evenly on top of mix. Pour melted butter evenly over nuts and mix. Do not stir! Bake for 30 minutes and serve warm with ice cream, if desired.

Option 2:

Substitute chocolate cake mix for the white and walnuts for the pecans. Follow all other instructions exactly.

Kingdom Come Chocolate Crescents

Be of Good Cheer Choco-Brownie Bars

Kingdom Come Chocolate Crescents

Ingredients:

1 pkg refrigerator crescent rolls
24 chocolate kisses
powdered sugar for dusting

Directions:

Preheat oven to 375F°.

Open and separate crescent roll dough into 8 triangles.
Place two chocolate kisses side-by-side on the wide end
of each triangle. Starting at wide end, roll dough to
opposite point. Pinch and seal edges

Place rolls on cookie sheet, point side down. Bend into a
crescent shape and bake for 10 minutes or golden
brown. Dust with powdered sugar and serve warm.

Be of Good Cheer Choco-Brownie Bars

Ingredients:

1 18oz pkg refrigerated chocolate chip cookie dough
1 box brownie mix
2 eggs
1 cup chopped nuts (walnuts or pecans)
¼ cup water
1/3 cup oil
1/2 cup chocolate chips

Directions:

Preheat oven to 350F°.

Coat a 9x11 baking dish with non-stick cooking spray. Press cookie dough evenly into bottom of pan.

In large bowl, stir together brownie mix, eggs, nuts, water, and oil. Pour batter evenly over cookie dough. Bake for 55 minutes or until brownies are firm on the edges and slightly gooey in the middle.

Place chocolate chips in a small microwave safe bowl and cook for 1 minute. Stir until smooth and drizzle over brownies.

Miraculous Mini-Cheesecakes

Miraculous Mini-Cheesecakes

Ingredients:

20 vanilla wafers, crushed
½ cup sugar
2 eggs
2 8oz pkgs cream cheese, softened
1 tsp vanilla

Directions:

Preheat oven to 325F°.

Line a muffin tin with foil cupcake liners. Distribute crushed wafers evenly among the 12 liners. Set aside.

In a large mixing bowl, beat cream cheese, vanilla and sugar on medium speed until well-blended. Add eggs and mix well. Pour batter over wafer crumbs until each liner is ¾ filled. Bake for 25 minutes. Remove from oven, let cool and then chill in refrigerator.

Before serving, top with strawberry slices and preserves.

Mountain High Monkey Pops

Ingredients:

3 ripe bananas, cut in half
6 popsicle sticks or bamboo skewers cut to size
1 cup semi-sweet or dark chocolate chips
1 Tbsp shortening
sprinkles

Directions:

Line a baking sheet with waxed paper. Carefully skewer each banana in the flat end. Place on baking sheet and put in freezer for one hour.

In microwave-safe bowl, combine chocolate chips and shortening. Melt in microwave on high, stirring after one minute. Cook in 10 second intervals, stirring each time, until smooth and shiny. Dip frozen bananas in chocolate and roll in sprinkles. Chill until set.

Angelic Angel Food Cake Macaroons

Glory Hallelujah Healthy Bites

Angelic Angel Food Cake Macaroons

Ingredients:

1 pkg angel food cake mix
½ cup water
1 ½ tsp almond extract or vanilla
2 cups flaked coconut

Directions:

Preheat oven to 350F°.

In large mixing bowl, beat cake mix, water and almond extract (or vanilla) on low speed for one minute to blend. Increase speed to medium and beat for 3 minutes until well blended. Add coconut and fold into batter.

With a melon-baller or tablespoon, drop dough onto greased cookie sheet. Bake for 8 to 10 minutes until set and slightly golden on tips. Cool on pan before removing.

Glory Hallelujah Healthy Bites

Ingredients:

1/3 cup dried cranberries
1/3 cup cheerios (plain or honey-nut)
1/3 cup chopped walnuts or pecans
1/3 cup coconut flakes
1/3 cup sunflower seeds
2 cups peanuts
1 cup semi-sweet or dark chocolate chips
1/3 cup honey
½ cup peanut butter

Directions:

In a large microwave-safe mixing bowl, melt chocolate chips on high for one minute, stir until smooth. If not melted, cook in 10 second intervals, stirring each time until smooth. Add peanut butter and honey and stir until creamy.

Add all remaining ingredients, stir until well mixed. Roll into 2" balls. Store in a plastic container with a lid in the refrigerator for up to one week.

Grand Graham Cracker Candy Bars

Fellowship Fudge

Grand Graham Cracker Candy Bars

Ingredients:

14 graham crackers
1 cup butter
1 cup brown sugar
1 12oz bag of dark chocolate chips
1 cup walnuts, chopped

Directions:

Preheat oven to 325F°.

Coat a cookie sheet with non-stick cooking spray and cover with one layer of graham crackers. Set aside.

In a medium saucepan melt butter with brown sugar. Bring to a boil over medium-high heat and boil for 2 minutes stirring constantly. Pour evenly over graham crackers and bake for 10 minutes.

Remove from oven and sprinkle with chocolate chips. Spread melting chips evenly over crackers. Top with walnuts. Cool, then cut into individual pieces.

Fellowship Fudge

Ingredients:

½ cup butter
1 6oz pkg of semi-sweet, dark or milk chocolate chips
1 tsp vanilla
2 cups sugar
1 5oz can evaporated milk (not condensed)
10 marshmallows, large
½ cup chopped walnuts, if desired

Directions:

Coat an 8x8 baking pan with non-stick cooking spray. (Or line with parchment paper.) Set aside.

In a large mixing bowl, place butter, chocolate chips and vanilla. Set aside.

In a medium saucepan, combine sugar, milk and marshmallows. Cook over medium heat until boiling, stirring constantly. Reduce heat to low and cook for another 5-6 minutes, still stirring constantly.

Pour hot mixture over contents of mixing bowl. Beat with an electric mixer until well blended. Fudge will be thick and dull looking. Stir in nuts. Pour into prepared square pan. Refrigerate until firm.

Count Your Blessings
Cookie-in-a-Mug

Count Your Blessings Cookie-in-a-Mug

Ingredients:

1 Tbsp butter
1 Tbsp brown sugar
3 drops vanilla
1 pinch of salt
1 egg yolk
¼ cup flour
2 Tbsp chocolate chips

Directions:

In a large coffee mug, melt butter in microwave (about 45 seconds). Stir in all remaining ingredients in order. Microwave for 40 – 60 seconds until cookie is done.

Top with mint ice cream (or any flavor you like) and serve immediately.

Lots of Love Lemonade Pie

Freewill Frothy Orange Drink

Lots of Love Lemonade Pie

Ingredients:

1 16 oz container of frozen whipped topping
1 6oz can of frozen lemonade
¾ cup lemon juice
2 cans sweetened condensed milk (not evaporated)
2 ready-made graham cracker crust pie shells

Directions:

In large mixing bowl, beat topping, lemonade, lemon juice and milk on medium until creamy and smooth. Pour evenly into the two pie shells. Refrigerate for 2 hours before serving.

Freewill Frothy Orange Drink

Ingredients:

1 6oz can frozen orange juice
1 cup water
1 cup milk
½ cup sugar
1 tsp vanilla
10 ice cubes

Directions:

Place all ingredients in blender and mix on high until thick and frothy. Do not over blend. Makes 4 servings.

Peanut Butter Recipes

(If you are allergic to peanut butter, substitute sunflower seed butter or pumpkin seed butter in these recipes, but please check with your physician or allergist first!)

Peanut Butter and Banana on Rice Cakes

Peanut Butter and Jelly Wrap

Got Peanut Butter?

-Serve it up on a rice cake and top it with banana slices.

-Roll peanut butter and jelly up in a tortilla to make a delicious wrap.

-Make an open faced sandwich on whole wheat or sprouted bread. Spread one slice of bread with peanut butter and top with sliced strawberries and bananas.

-Slice a banana. Take one slice, add a dollop of peanut butter, cover with another slice. Repeat to make poppers. Eat fresh or place on a cookie sheet and freeze. When frozen remove from pan and store in freezer bag in freezer until ready to pop 'em in your mouth.

-Remember 'Ants on a Log'? Take celery stalks and stuff them with peanut butter. Then top with raisins, nuts, or chocolate chips. (Or use all three!)

Peanut Butter, Strawberries and Bananas on Sprouted Bread

Peanut Butter Banana Poppers

Raisin Ants on a Log

Chocolate Chip Ants on a Log

PBJ Smoothie

-Make a PBJ protein smoothie. In a blender, place 2-3 tablespoons of peanut butter, 1-2 tablespoons jelly or jam, 1 scoop protein powder, 1 cup ice and 1 cup milk, yogurt, or ice cream. Blend until creamy and frothy.

-Make a dip by stirring ½ cup peanut butter with 1-2 tablespoons of honey. Stir until creamy and serve with apple wedges.

-Dip carrots and celery into plain peanut butter for a quick, healthy snack.

-Toast two freezer waffles. Take one and spread with peanut butter and top with banana slices. Place 2nd waffle on top. Drizzle with maple syrup, if desired.

-Toast a bagel. Spread both sides with peanut butter and top with thin apple slices. Sprinkle with cinnamon. Serve open-faced.

Apples with Peanut Butter Honey Dip

Carrots and Celery with Peanut Butter

Peanut Butter Banana Waffles

Toasted Bagel with Peanut Butter
and Apple Slices

Peanut Butter Fork Appetizers

PBJ with Pineapple and Banana

-Make fun peanut butter fork appetizers. Take a fork, spear fresh mint leaf, a banana slice topped with peanut butter, and cap with a strawberry. Repeat.

-Out of forks? Make spoon appetizers by dipping several spoons (plastic is great for parties) in peanut butter and place on a serving platter. Now top each with one of these toppings to create a fun variety of flavor bites:
a raspberry, a blueberry, a chocolate kiss, a cube of cheese, some coconut flakes, some raisins, mini-chocolate chips, a cheese puff or one slice of jalapeno, strawberry, or pickle. These are surprisingly delicious!

-Amp up your peanut butter, jelly and banana sandwich by adding a slice of pineapple or by grilling it. To grill spread a small amount of butter to both sides of sandwich and cook over medium heat in a small skillet until golden brown and crispy.

-Take a store-bought cupcake (or make box cupcakes according to package directions, cool) and slice in half, separating top from bottom. Spread bottom with your favorite jam or jelly, replace top, apply a dollop of peanut butter and top with a dash of jelly.

Grilled PBJ and Banana

PBJ Cupcake

Helpful Hints

School Wall Calendar

Although your cell phone can help you keep track of school assignments, due dates, birthdays, etc., making an 'old-fashioned' paper wall calendar can be extremely useful for college. Not only is it helpful to see a whole month of information hanging on the wall right in front of you, but the process of making the calendar will help you remember important dates and assignments as well. Let's begin:

-Purchase a school-year (August–August) calendar with large date squares. Highlighters can very helpful.

-When filling in the days, remember to write small as you may have several things due on each day. You can use the highlighters to denote certain classes (blue for history, yellow for math, etc.) or events (orange for birthdays, green for sporting events) and so on.

-Hang it on the wall over your desk – or somewhere else that you are sure to see it every day.

Before the semester begins:

-Go through your calendar and write down youth group meetings, church services and Bible studies.

-Next, go through the calendar and write down important family dates: birthdays, Mother's Day, Father's Day, family vacations or events. As you write something down, decide if there is an action you need to take in advance. If so, count back the number of days you need to prepare for the event and write in what you need to do. For example, when you enter Father's Day, count back five days and write 'mail Father's Day card' or 'buy gift for dad'.

-Look up your school's academic schedule. Write down all of the important registration dates: tuition due, last day to withdraw from classes, vacation days, when to register for next semester, etc.

-Look up your school's events schedule. Write down any sporting events, plays, concerts or guest lectures that you would like to attend. Do the same for dorm activities. (Write these small at the bottom of the day, leaving room for assignments and tests).

-If you are in an apartment, write down when your rent and utility bills are due. Count back five days from each entry and write, 'rent due in five days' or 'mail electric bill today', etc.

After the semester begins:

-On the first day of each new class, take down your calendar and put it side-by-side with the syllabus from that class. Go through the syllabus line-by-line and write on your calendar when all assignments are due and the dates of all quizzes, tests, oral arguments, etc.

-For every test, count back one week and write, 'test next week'. Then count back another week and write 'test in two weeks'. Go back as far as you would like.

-Repeat the above steps for all term paper and research paper due dates. Make sure you end up with something like this: History paper due in six weeks, make outline and find resources. History paper due in five weeks, research! History paper due in four weeks, finish rough draft. History paper due in three weeks, fix rough areas, flesh out weak spots. History paper due in two weeks, finish final copy, run it by professor. History paper due in one week – reread, make sure it is ready. History paper due today!

-Schedule your reading assignments and any new assignments as soon as you get them, counting backwards and scheduling your plan to complete them on time.

Having a plan, seeing it in writing every day, and following through will give you peace of mind that you are on the right track for a successful year!

Make a Weekly Menu:

Before you head out to the grocery store, you should plan your meals for the week. This way you can make sure you have all of the ingredients that you need for each day. It will save you time and money if you only shop once a week. If you run back and forth to the store for missing ingredients, chances are you will impulse buy a bunch of other things that you don't really need.

Making a weekly menu will also save you money because you can plan different meals that use some of the same ingredients. One night's leftovers is the next nights main course if you add just a few things to change it up.

For example, the leftover pecan-crusted salmon from Monday night can become Tuesday's fish tacos. Leftover sausage from breakfast burritos becomes stuffed empanadas for dinner. Leftover salad greens become stuffing for a Chicken Caesar Wrap. Tortillas for your breakfast burritos are the wraps for your chicken caesar.

Frozen berries can be used in smoothies, yogurt parfaits, and blueberry muffins. You need milk for cereal, but also the pecan crusted salmon and potato soup. Pecans can be used in the pecan-crusted salmon, chicken salad and homemade granola.

Another time saver is cooking all of your meat at the beginning of the week. Brown a pound of hamburger and store individual servings in sandwich bags in the refrigerator. When you are in a hurry, take out a serving to make tacos, nachos or to stuff a potato. Add some leftover spaghetti sauce and dollop on leftover rolls to make Sloppy Joes.

Bake or grill a package of boneless chicken breasts and wrap each in foil and store in refrigerator. For a quick dinner, take one out, cut it into cubes and make a chicken taco, a tossed chicken salad or a wrap.

To begin your menu, take a piece of paper and write down the days of the week. Look through this cookbook and others (or online) and choose meals that sound good to you. Make a list of ingredients for each dish and compare them to each other.

Now plug the meals into each day of the week keeping in mind the leftover/common ingredients ideas we just went over. Use the recipe ingredients to make your grocery list. Keep in mind the things you already have on hand.

Add some vegetables for side dishes and fruit and yogurt for snacking. Skip the soda and plan on drinking water or home-brewed ice tea (add tea bags to your list).

Keep a piece of paper on or next to the fridge to write down ingredients as you run out of them during the week. Add these things to next week's shopping.

A few more tips:

-Make a menu with your roommates and shop together so you can split the bill.

-Assign a night or two to each roommate where they are responsible for cooking dinner and cleaning up. You will learn new recipes from each other and have a few nights a week where you can focus on studying while someone else cooks.

-If you do make separate meals, trade leftovers with your roommates so you get a variety of food.

-You can easily freeze pancakes, muffins and bread and take them out as you need them. Thaw on counter or microwave for a few seconds and they are ready to eat.

First Trip to the Grocery Store:

On your first trip to the store, you will need to purchase pantry staples. These are flour, white sugar, brown sugar, vanilla, baking powder, baking soda, olive oil, canola oil, honey, cooking spray, low-sodium chicken broth and bread crumbs. Don't forget the peanut butter!

You will need various spices as you try new recipes, so if you can afford to, invest in a pre-stocked spice rack. Otherwise, buy one or two spices each time you go to the store. The most commonly used spices in recipes are salt, pepper, garlic powder, onion powder, cinnamon, nutmeg, paprika, dried mustard and chili powder.

For dessert-making you will need to buy a small can of shortening, chocolate chips, flaked coconut and a bag of powdered sugar.

In the fridge, you will need milk, eggs, a jar of hot sauce, Worcestershire sauce, mayo, mustard, peppers, olives, pickles, jam and butter. Don't forget lunch meat, cheese, salad greens, and a red onion. For quick healthy snacks buy string cheese, hummus, yogurt and fruit. (Buy fresh or frozen fruit and vegetables. These have the most nutrients. Skip the canned if possible.)

On this first trip you will need to buy cleaning supplies (rubber gloves, glass cleaner, disinfectant cleaner or wipes, floor cleaner, laundry detergent, dishwasher soap, dish soap, paper towels), toilet paper and tissues. You will also need storage bags. A large box of sandwich bags and one box of gallon-sized freezer bags should be a good start.

Grocery Store Tips:

-Try to go shopping only once a week. Every time you go into the store you will be tempted to pick up extra items that you don't really need.

- Go with a prepared grocery list for the week. Stick to this list. Buy only what you need and do not get tempted by displays and samples for things you do not.

-The best day of the week to shop for groceries is usually Wednesday. Most stores start their new promotions on this day. Check with your store to see when they put out the new ads.

-Look for coupons in the newspaper and online and don't be afraid to use them. They are money in your pocket.

-Stick to the outer aisles of the store. This is where you will find the fresh fruit and dairy, the deli, and the bakery. The middle aisles contain the boxed and canned processed foods that are not good for you.

-Buy generic brands of over-the-counter medicines. Pain relief, cough and cold, and allergy medicines usually contain the exact same ingredients for much less than the name brands. Read and compare labels.

-You can also buy generic salt, sugar, spices and some cereals. Paper products and storage bags can be iffy so try generic in these once and decide for yourself if they are worth it.

-**Hamburger**: The percentages on ground beef refer to the fat content. For tacos, spaghetti sauce, and Sloppy Joes, buy 90/10. It is healthier for you and the spices will make up for the lack of fat. For hamburger patties go with 80/20. They will have better flavor and they won't be dry. Avoid the 70/30. 30% fat is too much! The meat should be bright pink to red and have no odor. (If you can afford it look for organic ground beef.)

-**Roast**: When buying a roast for your crock pot, you can purchase the cheaper cuts of beef. These are usually less tender, but slow-cooking them all day makes up for this. When you graduate and start making the big bucks, you can move up to the more expensive stuff! A quick way to compare quality is to look at the *per pound* price, not the overall price. If one roast is $1.21 per pound and the next one is $1.35 per pound, the second one is considered a better cut of meat. Here are a few of the more common roasts:

-*Chuck*: fatty and tough, but works well in a crock pot. Chuck roasts can include shoulder, top blade, cross rib, arm and 7-bone.

-*Round*: cheap and lean, not real tender, also best in crock pot or other slow-cooking method in moisture. These include: top round, bottom round, London Broil, eye of round.

Rib Roast: juicy and tender cuts, but also more expensive. These are usually baked in the oven at a low temperature over a few hours. They include: standing rib roast and prime rib.

-*Sirloin*: tender, lean and pricier than most. These include bottom and top butt and tri-tip. Great for grilling!

-*Short loin*: the most expensive, but also the best tasting and most tender. These include: top loin and tenderloin. The better the cut the less cooking time, moisture and spices needed. You don't want to hide the flavor, that's what you paid for!

-**Fish**: Buying fish is really a matter of taste as well as budget. There are different studies on the matter, some say that wild-caught fish are better for you than farmed fish, but you will pay more for them. As with anything else food-wise, buy the best that you can afford and move on. Don't break the bank trying to keep up with ever-changing food studies! Buy fish fresh or frozen. Cook fresh fish right away. Thaw frozen fish overnight (in its original packaging) in the refrigerator only, not on kitchen counter! Rinse all fish with cold water and pat dry before cooking. The most common table fish are:

Talapia: a mild, flaky, white tropical fish. Very affordable and tasty. You can bake them with or without sauce and use them in many different recipes.

Halibut: a dense and firm fish with a very mild taste. They are usually baked, grilled or batter-fried. They are also on the more expensive side.

Salmon: a red/orange, dense and oily fish. They have a fishier taste than white fish, but are still considered to be mild. They are also higher in omega-3 oils. Salmon is usually baked or grilled. About the same price-wise as the halibut.

Cod: white, moist and flaky, they are the most affordable fish on this list. They are usually used to make fish and chips, fish sticks, etc. They are mild in flavor and best when battered and deep fried.

-**Chicken**: Buy fresh or frozen chicken thighs and boneless chicken breasts. Read the labels and buy brands that are government inspected, grade A. The skin should be white to yellow in color. The meat should not be pasty or gray and should not have an odor. The thighs will be fatter, but have more flavor. The breasts are healthier for you, but can sometimes become dry and chewy when overcooked. Rinse each piece with cold water and pat dry before cooking. Wash your hands and disinfect all surfaces after handling chicken. Cook completely until the meat is no longer pink and the juices run clear.

-**Organic**: If you can afford it, try to buy the following fruits and vegetables from the organic section of your grocery store: strawberries, grapes, cherries, nectarines, raspberries, pears, peaches, apples, celery, potatoes, and spinach leaves. They have been grown without pesticides and GMOs. Things that have a hard or thick rind or skin (melons, for example) do not need to be organic.

-**How to choose a ripe:**

Cantaloupe – Make sure it feels firm, not mushy. The rind should be more white and orange than white and green. Smell the stem end, it should smell fresh and fruity, like a cantaloupe. If it has no smell or smells like mold, skip it. Wash rind thoroughly with soap and water before slicing.

Watermelon – Pick one with bright colored skin and a symmetrical shape. Make sure there are no dents or bruises on it. Put it to your ear and thump it with your finger. If it sounds thick put it back, if it sounds hollow it is ripe. Wash rind thoroughly with soap and water before slicing.

Avocado – Hold it in the palm of your hand and gently squeeze, if it gives slightly it is ready. If it is mushy or easily dented it is over-ripe. If it does not give at all it will be ready in a few days. Color helps as well: medium green means ripe, dark brownish green means overripe and bright green means not quite ready. Wash the skin before slicing.

Pineapple – Look for one that has a lighter color around the base, it should feel heavy for its size and smell sweet. If it only smells sweet on one end, it is just starting to ripen. It will smell sweet from top to bottom when fully ripe. Wash before slicing.

Grapes – Grapes should be bright colored, plump and unblemished. They should be firmly attached to a healthy looking, flexible, light brown or green stem. They should be stored in the refrigerated aisle of the fruits and vegetables section. It is hard to judge sweetness based on looks, so if the store offers samples, taste one before buying the bunch.

Bananas – Ripe bananas are yellow all over, firm but not hard and have a sweet smell. Make sure they do not have bruises or blemishes on the peel. They ripen quickly, so do not buy more than you can use in a few days or buy a few slightly green ones to eat later on as they ripen.

Dining Out:

Here are a few tips to help you save money on those rare occasions when you get to eat out:

-When ordering a frozen or iced coffee drink from a well-known coffee shop, get the grande size and ask them to put it into two cups. You and a friend will save a lot of money over ordering two separate 'talls'.

-Most restaurants have certain days when they offer specials. Usually these are at the beginning of the week. Call or look up the restaurants in your area find out which nights are 'deal' nights.

-Always check online for coupons.

-Do not order soda or tea. The mark-up is outrageous. Order ice water and bring your own cold-brew tea bag or order it with several lemon slices. Squeeze the lemon into the water and add sugar or sweetener and you have fresh-squeezed lemonade – for free.

-If you do order a drink, and it does not come with refills, (specialty lemonades, etc.) order it without ice. Then ask for a glass of ice on the side. You will get twice as much.

-The portion sizes are huge, so ask for a to-go box when your food comes. Immediately put half of your meal into the box. Now you have dinner for tomorrow, as well. If you wait until the end of dinner to get the box you might be tempted to clean your plate. Don't forget the leftover rolls in the bread basket.

-If you are dining with a friend, order two salads and split one entree. You will have plenty of food for less money.

-Look for other ways to split with friends. For example, at a famous wings place a snack size portion gets you 4-5 wings. For just a couple of dollars more, you can get the small size which gets you 8-10 pieces. If you split the small with a friend you get the same amount of food as two snack sizes for a lot less money.

-Do you want a steak dinner for less? Order a steak salad with the steak on the side or a steak sandwich, no bun, with a baked potato instead of fries. You will usually get the same amount of food as their steak dinner, but it will cost less just because of the way it was ordered.

-Order your entree from the appetizer menu. Add a salad or a bowl of soup and you have a filling meal for less money.

Is There a Method to this Madness?
(or How to Clean Your Room)

You didn't mean for it to happen, but here you are again staring into the chaotic, clutter-filled nether-world that used to be your dorm room. You had such good intentions when you first moved in. You were going to be organized and your room was going to represent the new, fastidious, uncluttered you. But with classes, homework and social time things got away from you and your room became the perfect example for your physics paper on entropy.

In fact, just thinking about trying to clean it sends you running to the nearest coffee shop so you can hide inside a grande, non-fat, extra hot, mocha cappucinno.

Well, never fear. There is an order to everything in the Universe and fortunately for you, your room is in the Universe! So here are a few tips to make this task seem less onerous:

-Do not look at the room as a whole. You will get discouraged. Instead, take things one step at a time, only focusing on the task at hand. When you have completed everything in a step, you can move on to the next one.

-Put on some music, but do not turn on your television or computer. Something to listen to is great! Something that makes you keep looking at it is not.

-Gather your supplies before you begin. If you leave your room to get something after you have started cleaning, there is a 92.7% chance that you will not return. Get a garbage bag, a dust rag, glass cleaner, paper towels and a vacuum cleaner or broom.

You are now ready to begin!

-First things first – make your bed. If there are piles of stuff on it move them to the floor. We will get to them in a minute. A made bed immediately makes the room look better and it gives you a flat service to sort things on.

-Pick up each piece of loose clothing. Look at it, smell it. Is it clean? Put it away. Is it dirty? Put it in the hamper (if it is stained, spray it with stain remover before you drop it into the hamper). This step usually takes the longest, but do not move on until every last piece of clothing is in its proper place. (This goes for shoes, too!)

-Take your garbage bag (or two if you have recycling) and pick up and discard all garbage. Don't forget to check under the bed! That forgotten banana peel won't smell very good in a few days! Place the bag(s) outside your door. Do not leave! Go on to next task.

-Pick up all dirty dishes. Stack them outside the door next to your garbage bag(s).

-Now gather up all school supplies, books and papers. Lay them on top of your bed and sort them in order of importance and according to due dates. Put them neatly on your desk in a way that makes sense to you.

-Now pick up anything that is left (jewelry, hair ties, video game controllers, toiletries, etc.) and put them where they belong.

-Take the dusting rag and run it over all flat surfaces. Clean your mirror and window with the glass cleaner and paper towels. Vacuum or sweep your floor.

-Take your garbage out to the dumpster and your dishes to the kitchen. Wash and put them away immediately.

-Pat yourself on the back and go enjoy your clean haven with that extra hot mocha cappucinno!

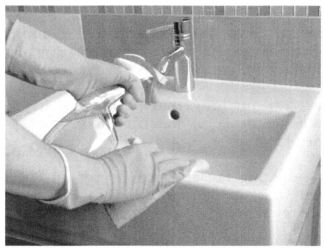

How to Clean Your Bathroom

Depending on your living situation, you may have a bathroom that you have to keep clean. As with your bedroom, there is a system that can help you whip through this decidedly un-fun chore and get back to your life. Here it is:

-Gather everything you will need: rubber gloves, glass cleaner, paper towels, Clorox wipes, disinfecting bathroom cleaner, sponge, toilet brush, broom.

-Put all loose items and toiletries away into drawers or the linen closet.

-Pick up dirty towels and throw them into your hamper. (If they are wet, wash them right away or hang to dry before putting them into your hamper.)

-Put on your gloves.

-Spray cleaner in sink, bathtub and on the tile surrounding the tub. Also, spray inside the toilet bowl. Let soak.

-Clean mirror with glass cleaner and paper towels.

-Take the sponge and scrub the sink. Rinse.

-Wipe down the counter top with a Clorox wipe or with the disinfecting spray and a paper towel.

-Using the sponge, scrub the bathtub and tile. Rinse thoroughly. Rinse and wring out the sponge.

-Take your toilet brush and swish it around inside of the toilet bowl, scrubbing it clean. Don't forget to brush under the rim.

-Clean the outside of the toilet in this order:
a. get a Clorox wipe and clean the water tank, top and sides
b. wipe the lid, top and bottom, leave lid up
c. wipe the seat, top and bottom, leave seat up
d. get a new wipe and clean the area of the bowl where the lid is attached to the rim, clean well around screws and then clean the rest of the rim.
e. get a new wipe and clean all around the outside of the bowl, where the bowl is attached to the floor, and the floor around the toilet. Discard all wipes.

-Empty the garbage.

-Turn on bath tub faucet and wash your gloved hands with soap and hot water. Remove gloves and lay them on the side of the tub with the sponge to dry.

-Sweep and mop your floor if necessary.

-Put supplies away and get back to your life!

Laundry Stinks!
(in more ways than one)

We hate doing laundry! We love wearing clean clothes! Enough said, let's get it done!

-Make sure you have a laundry basket or hamper to throw dirty clothes into. Keep a bottle of stain remover and a delicates bag in or next to basket/hamper.

-When you change clothes, put cast-offs immediately into hamper. This takes approximately 2 seconds and will save you time later since you won't have to clean your room as often.

-Spray stains with spot remover when you put them into hamper. This will keep the stains from setting and you won't have to remember what was stained and what wasn't on laundry day. Put delicates directly into delicates bag so you won't have to dig for them later.

-When you are ready to wash clothes, sort into piles accordingly: dark colors, light colors, whites, jeans, sheets and towels. Do not wash jeans with other clothes because they will beat them up with their rough fabric and hardware. Towels can sometimes be washed with clothes, but they can transfer soap and body oils to the more delicate fabrics. Try to wash your sheets once a week.

-Read the washing instruction labels on your clothes when you purchase them. Some things need to be hand washed, washed in a certain temperature, or dry cleaned. Keep this is mind when sorting.

-To hand wash delicates, buy a bottle of hand-washing detergent. Now just follow the instructions on bottle. Basically it involves filling your sink with cool water and one capful of detergent. Place delicates in water and gently massage them until clean. Rinse thoroughly. Gently wring out excess water and lie flat on a towel or hang over a shower bar to dry.

-To machine wash clothes, read the instructions inside the lid on the machine. It will tell you where to put your laundry detergent. Read the instructions on your detergent label to find out how much to use. These vary from machine to machine and detergent to detergent.

-Wash sorted piles one at a time accordingly: dark colors in cold water, light colors in warm, jeans in warm, whites in hot and towels and sheets in hot.

-When clean, transfer clothes to dryer. Add a fabric softener sheet and dry on low temp for 10 minutes. Now pull out anything delicate, all shirts, dresses, leggings and khakis. Hang these on hangers or over shower curtain bar to dry. If you do this, your clothes will keep their color and shape for much longer than if you put them all in the dryer. Also, most of them will dry wrinkle-free. Dry remaining colors and whites for an additional 30 minutes. Towels and jeans may take longer.

-Fold clothes immediately after drying, while they are still warm. If you wait until you get back to your room to fold them the heat will set the wrinkles and you will end up having to iron.

-Finish up by putting everything into its proper drawer or closet. Great job!

Individual Study:

Read and pray over these verses.
How can you apply them to your life as a
college student and beyond?

Pray without ceasing,
1 Thessalonians 5:17 ESV

Cast all your anxiety on him because he cares for you.
1 Peter 5:7 NIV

For the wages of sin is death, but the gift of God is
eternal life through Jesus Christ our Lord.
Romans 6:23 KJV

Devotion Index:

Feed Your Mind and Your Spirit...6
Do Clothes Really Make the (Wo)Man...7
Take My Advice...please...8
The Heavyweight in Your Corner...9
Don't Tempt Me...10
Hey, Good Lookin'...11
That's Why They Call It Faith...12
Is There Someone Else I Can Talk To?...13
Give Thanks in All Circumstances...14
According to Your Gifts...15
Go Ahead, Ask...16
Who Are You?...17
A New Beginning...18
Watch Where You Point That Thing...19
A Great Story...20
Power...21
Say It Now...22
Keeping It Positive...23
Rain on My Parade, please...24
It's Not Just About You...25
Gear Up...26
Increase Your Odds...27
Forgive and Forget...28
Aaah, My Eyes, My Eyes...29
Sing His Praises...30
What's Old Is New Again...31
Pushing Forward...32
Enemy Mine...33

Well, I Didn't Vote For Him...34
There Ain't No Rhyme for Consequences...35
Don't Skip to the End...36
More Than You Can Handle...37
Banana, Anyone?...38
Represent...39
One Is Silver and the Other is Gold...40
Now, That's a Big S.E.P. Field!...41
This Too Shall Pass...42
What if God Was One of Us?...43
My Body is a What?...44
The Words in Red...45
You are in Good Hands...46
Unshakeable...47
Weakness to Strength...48
Asking With Confidence...49
Good and Plenty...50
Restoration for the Weary...51
Faith Like a River...52
The Future's So Bright I Have to Wear Shades...53
You Catch More Unicorns With Rainbows...54
Promises, Promises...55
It's a Marathon, Not a Sprint...56
Enough Said...57
The Past Has Passed...58
God is Good...59
The Best Medicine...60
When In Doubt, Pray It Out...61
Read It Again, for the First Time...62
Keep Moving Heavenward...63

Make the Commitment...64
Make Your Words Count...65
Praise Ye the Lord, Hallelujah...66
God As Man...67
Mountain Strong...68
The Foundation's the Thing...69
Listen Carefully...70
Don't Forget the Guidebook...71
Do Not Despair...72
Teach Me to Pray...73
Love Bigger Than Yourself...74
The Support Team Could Use Some Support...75
Random Acts...76
Us vs. Them...77
Keep Calm and Carry On...78
S.O.S....79
Actions Speak Louder...80
The Lord is My Sherpa...81
Bad Day at Black Rock...82
Eternally Yours...83
He Cares For You...84
Is the Futon Ready?...85
It Keeps Going and Going...86
True Love...87
Dig In...88
God Don't Make No Junk...89
Genuine Genuflection...90
Safe Haven...91
Hang in There, Baby!...92
True Value...93

He Walked a Mile In Your Sandals...94
The Way...95
The Truth...96
And The Life...97
Wear a Chest Protector...98
What Is A Million Dollars Worth?...99
But Will You?...100
Global Extreme Warming Ice Age...101
You Might Want to Walk that Back...102
Clean Up in Aisle Three...103
Return the Favor...104
The Best (Verse) for Last...105

Recipe Index:

Amen Apple Crisp...146
Angelic Angel Food Cookies...157
Be Bold Buckeyes...148
Be of Good Cheer Choco-Brownie Bars...152
Be Ye Fishers of Men Fish Tacos...128
Be Ye Gracious Granola...114
Bountiful Earth Blueberry Muffins...120
Brand New Day Breakfast Burritos...117
Brand New Life Broccoli Cheese Soup...130
Bring On the Glory Breakfast Sandwich...116
Champion Chicken Salad...150
Cherubic Cherry Smoothie...109
Count Your Blessing Cookie-in-a-Mug...163
Deliciously Devine Dump Cake...149
Evening Grace Easy Roast Beef...143
Fellowship Fudge...161
Freewill Frothy Orange Drink...166
Glory Hallelujah Healthy Bites...158
Grand Graham Cracker Candy Bars...160
Hope Eternal Honey Chicken...138
Inner Strength Straw and Hay...135
Kingdom Come Chocolate Crescents...151
Lead the Charge Chicken Caesar Wrap...133
Lots of Love Lemonade Pie...165
Mighty Mandarin and Grape Tossed Salad...136
Miraculous Mini Cheesecakes...154
Mountain High Monkey Pops...155
No More Fear Not-Fried Chicken...139

Peanut Butter Recipes...167-178
Positive Attitude Potato Cheese Soup...131
Pray for Peace Pecan Crusted Salmon or Halibut...141
Prayer and Peanut Butter Pancakes...119
Revel and Rejoice Ramen...144
Stand Firm Stuffed Micro-Baked Potato...126
Steadfast Sticky Buns...123
Sweet Embrace Empanadas...122
Veritable Veritas Veggie Scramble...111
Youthful Yogurt Parfait...113

Helpful Hints Index:

School Wall Calendar...180
Make a Weekly Menu...183
First Trip to the Grocery Store...186
Grocery Store Tips...188
Dining Out...193
How to Clean Your Room...195
How to Clean Your Bathroom...198
Laundry Stinks...200

Made in the USA
Coppell, TX
04 June 2022

78468099R00118